EXTENDING

Word *for* Windows

Carol McKenzie • Pat Bryden

Heinemann

Heinemann Educational
a division of Heinemann Publishers (Oxford) Ltd,
Halley Court, Jordan Hill, Oxford OX2 8EJ

OXFORD LONDON EDINBURGH MADRID ATHENS BOLOGNA
PARIS MELBOURNE SYDNEY AUCKLAND SINGAPORE TOKYO
IBADAN NAIROBI HARARE GABORONE PORTSMOUTH NH (USA)

© Carol McKenzie and Patricia Bryden 1995

First Published 1995

95 96 97 98 11 10 9 8 7 6 5 4 3 2 1

A catalogue record for this book is available from the British Library on request.

ISBN 0 435 454196

Designed by Raynor Design using QuarkXPress 3.3™ on the Apple Macintosh™

Printed in Great Britain by Thomson Litho Ltd, East Kilbride, Scotland

Screen shots reprinted with permission from Microsoft Corporation

Contents

About this book

Extending Word for Windows has been written as a continuation text to *Introducing Word for Windows* by the same authors. It has been designed as a progressive course and is suitable for use in the classroom, in an open-learning workshop or as a private study aid.

Extending Word for Windows will help those preparing to take an intermediate examination in word processing, using Word for Windows. However, the book would be equally useful to those who simply wish to extend their working knowledge of word processing.

The syllabuses covered include:

RSA Text Processing Stage II Part 1

RSA Word Processing Stage II Part 2

Pitman Examinations Institute Intermediate Word Processing

City & Guilds of London Institute Level 2

NVQ Administration Level 2 Units

Students will derive most benefit from this book by working through the units in the order they appear. It has been designed to be a progressive course.

Previous experience: It is assumed that you have completed an elementary (Stage I) word-processing course and are therefore familiar with conventional document layout and basic text-processing principles and practice. You should also be familiar with the hardware you are going to use (including the printer).

Format of the book

The book is divided into nine units, taking you through the word-processing functions you need to know for intermediate examinations. Instructions for the preparation of particular documents are given at the beginning of each unit, followed by information on the Word for Windows commands relevant to the functions you will use. Exercises within each unit allow you to put the knowledge into practice.

Consolidation practice for each stage of learning is included in Units 4 and 8.

Examination practice for each stage of learning is included in Unit 9. This practice has been designed to cover the requirements of examinations offered by RSA, Pitman Examinations Institute and the City & Guilds of London Institute.

Letterheads for use with the relevant exercises are provided for student use. These may be photocopied as necessary.

Print-out checks for all exercises are given at the back of the book. These should be used for checking by both students and teachers/trainers.

Command boxes for Word for Windows functions are given when appropriate. Instruction is given on how to carry out the required function. The commands are given for keyboard, mouse and menu users. Students may select their preferred method.

The progress review checklist allows students to keep a record of progress through the exercises, noting any comments on topics if necessary. If completed at the end of each working session, the student can refer to this checklist to locate without delay the unit to be worked next.

The glossary provides a comprehensive, alphabetically listed quick reference for all the Word for Windows commands introduced in the book. The commands are shown for keyboard, mouse and menu users.

How to use this book

If you are preparing for an examination, you are advised to work through the book unit by unit.

The book has been planned as a progressive course and some of the work you will do in the later units is based on text you will have keyed in earlier so *it is important to save your work.*

Working through a unit

1   When you see this symbol, read all the information before you begin. You may also need to refer back to this information as you carry out the exercises.

2   When you see this symbol, carry out the exercises, following the numbered steps, e.g. **1.1, 1.2**.

3   Use your spelling tool to check your document. Proof-read your document carefully – the spelling tool does not find every error.

4   Use the Print Preview facility to check that your document is going to be correct when printed. If it is, save your work on to your floppy disk (usually in A drive). Then print your work.

5   Compare your document with the print-out checks at the back of the book. (If you are using this book in class, your tutor may also wish to check your work.) Correct any errors which you find in your work. Print the documents again if required to do so by your tutor. (If you are working on your own, you may not consider this necessary.)

6   Complete your progress review checklist. Then exit from Word for Windows or begin work on the next unit (as appropriate).

Do not delete files from your disk – you will need them later!

Introduction to Word for Windows

Microsoft Windows is a graphical user interface which allows the user to communicate with the computer. The graphical nature of the messages on screen makes Windows a user-friendly operating system. *Word for Windows* is a software package used for text processing which operates within the Windows environment.

When you start the Word for Windows program, the following **document window** will be displayed on screen:

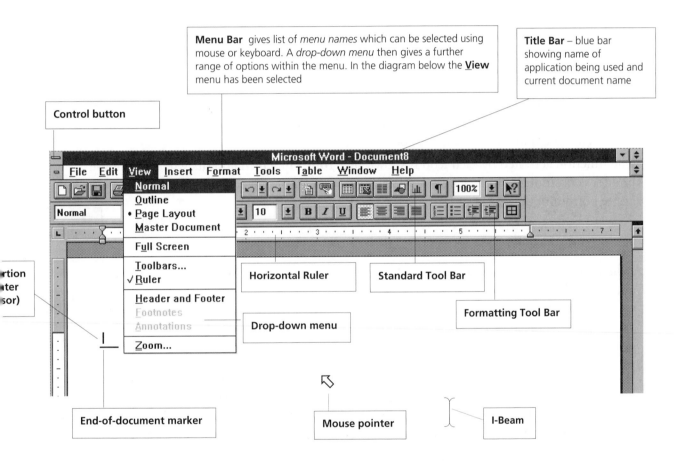

Menu Bar gives list of *menu names* which can be selected using mouse or keyboard. A *drop-down menu* then gives a further range of options within the menu. In the diagram below the **View** menu has been selected

Title Bar – blue bar showing name of application being used and current document name

Control button

Horizontal Ruler

Standard Tool Bar

Formatting Tool Bar

Drop-down menu

End-of-document marker

Mouse pointer

I-Beam

When Word is carrying out a function, it may ask you to wait. The icon for this is the **hourglass** ⧗. Wait until the hourglass has disappeared from the screen before proceeding with the next step.

The **status bar** at the bottom of the screen displays information about the document on screen, e.g. the page number, section number, line number, column number, etc. For example:

| Page 3 | Sec 1 | 3/3 | At 1″ | Ln 1 | Col 10 | 10:21 |

Menu

To select an option from the menu you can either:

- use the keyboard – press the underlined letter for the required menu option
- use the mouse – click the mouse pointer on the option required
- use a keyboard shortcut, e.g. **Ctrl** + **F** selects the **Find** menu option (holding down the **Ctrl** key and then pressing the letter shown will activate the command)

A **tick** against a menu choice indicates that the option is currently in operation. When the tick is removed, the facility is 'switched off'. An **ellipsis** after a menu choice (e.g. **Zoom** ...) indicates that you will be asked to give more information before the command can be executed.

Tool Bars

To select an icon from the Standard or Formatting Tool Bar you:

click: The mouse pointer ⤹ on the icon

Each icon on the Tool Bars represents a different function. For example, clicking on the Print icon would activate the printer to print a copy of the current document. The use of icons is explained more fully throughout the book.

The function activated by each icon is shown in a **Tool Tip** which appears when the mouse pointer is positioned on the icon. (A fuller description appears at the same time in the **status bar** at the bottom of the screen.)

The **Bold** Tool Tip

When you click on an icon button it is 'switched on' to show that the function is currently in operation.

Dialogue box

When Word needs to give or receive more information, a **dialogue box** is displayed on screen. You can move through the dialogue box using the **Tab** key or the **Arrow** keys on the keyboard, or you can use the mouse to move to the section you need. Word for Windows asks you to respond by presenting information, options or questions in different ways by using boxes and buttons (see below).

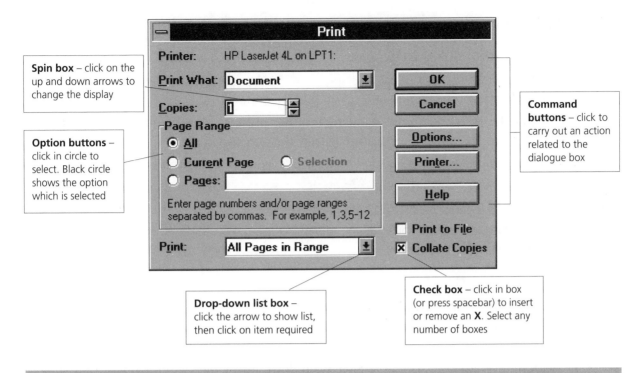

Spin box – click on the up and down arrows to change the display

Option buttons – click in circle to select. Black circle shows the option which is selected

Command buttons – click to carry out an action related to the dialogue box

Drop-down list box – click the arrow to show list, then click on item required

Check box – click in box (or press spacebar) to insert or remove an **X**. Select any number of boxes

The Scroll Bars

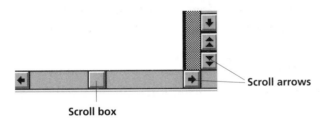

Scroll arrows

Scroll box

The **Scroll Bars** at the right side and bottom of the screen allow text to be scrolled by the use of the mouse, e.g. clicking on the [↓] button will move the 'document frame' downwards so that the text moves up the screen.

 Scroll Bar showing View buttons and left scroll button

The Scroll Bar also displays buttons to select the different ways in which a document can be viewed.

Using the mouse

The mouse is used to move a pointer to any required location on screen. The mouse has two buttons: **left** and **right**. As you move the mouse across the desk, an electronic sensor picks up the movement of the ball and moves the **mouse pointer** across the screen in the same direction.

* You use the mouse to *point* to the item you want on screen.
* You then *click* the mouse button (usually the left one) to highlight or *select* an option on screen (quickly pressing and releasing the button).
* Sometimes you *double-click* a mouse button (quickly pressing and releasing the button twice).
* You may also use a *dragging* action by holding down the mouse button, moving the mouse and then releasing the button.

The Help Menu

Word for Windows offers on-line **Help** to users. The help command can be activated in two ways from the document screen:

• By selecting **Help** from the menu bar

• By clicking on the ⬛ icon on the Standard Tool Bar and then clicking on the feature on screen or keying in the name of the feature with which you require help

Selecting **Contents** from the Help drop-down menu gives a list of the features available, e.g.:

Examples and Demos

Visual examples and demonstrations to help
you learn Word

Using Word

Step-by-step instructions to help you complete
your tasks

Selecting **Search for Help on ...** from the Help drop-down menu gives you the opportunity to key in the name of the feature with which you require help.

Selecting **Index** displays an alphabetical list of functions and features. You can move quickly through the list by clicking on the alphabetical button of the feature you require at the top of the index screen.

Selecting **Quick Preview** activates a learning program which introduces you to Word for Windows.

Selecting **Examples and Demos** allows you to access demonstrations of a range of Word features.

1 *Text editing*

At the end of Unit 1 you will have learnt how to
- *identify typographical and spelling errors in a printed document by comparing it against a manuscript original*
- *amend a document in accordance with correction signs*
- *expand abbreviations correctly*
- *change the line length for a document*

---

i | Typescript containing typographical errors

Text processing may involve correcting any mistakes made in previous print-outs. Watch out for uncorrected spelling errors and transposition errors. It is up to you to notice typographical errors, to decide what is wrong and to key in the text correctly.

Examples

This sentance contains <u>3 speling errers</u>.

should be keyed in as: **This sentence contains <u>3 spelling errors.</u>**

This sentence contians <u>2 transpositoin errors</u>.

should be keyed in as: **This sentence contains 2 <u>transposition errors.</u>**

The exercises in this book have been keyed in using the Arial font in point size 10. Please use this font and point size for your work.

Exercise 1A

1.1 Switch on and load Word for Windows.

1.2 Insert your work disk in the disk drive.

1.3 The following text contains 23 errors. The original manuscript on page 9 shows the document as it should be. Read through the passage, identifying the errors, and then key in a correct copy.

Note: Some words are in italics – use the Formatting Tool Bar **_I_** or **Ctrl + I** to obtain this.

PRODUCING PERFECT COPY

It is easy to think that, because you have used the spelling tool in Word, your work is accurate. Automatic spelling checks are very useful and you should always use it if it is available on your system, before you save or print a document but you must *also* proof read the document yourself.

Word's spelling facility compares each word you have keyed in with its own 'dictionary' of words.

Candidates who fail examinations often do because their proofreading is not adequate. One of the most common errors is the of words. Unfortunately, if you have missed out some words, or you have not deleted some words as instructed, spellchecking will not detcet this.

If you have typed the wrong version of a word, e.g. **there** instead of **their**, spelling check will not detect this as both versions are spelled correctly. However, Word's grammar tool should detect the error and suggest the correct version to you.

Only you can tell if you have copied names of places or people correctly and if a peice of information which you were asked to find is accurate. For example, spellcheck cannot tell if the date you have keyed in for 'Thursday of next week' is the correct one. Don't guess - use a diary or calendar. To check up on todays date, you could use Word's Date and Time facility which is found under the Insert Menu. (The current date is displayed on the Status Bar at the bottom of the screen.)

The skills of proof-reading are essential in text processing. You should train yourself to check every detail in work you have done before you print so as not to to waste paper. It is not enough to check the work on your screen, you must compaire it with the 'copy' from which you are working - going through it word by word.

1.4 Use the spelling and grammar tools to check your work, and proof-read it yourself carefully.

1.5 Save and print your document, using filename **EX1A**. Check your print-out with that at the back of the book. If you find any errors, correct them and print again if necessary.

(Producing Perfect Copy) ← CAPS & centre

Please put underlined words in italics and circled words in bold

It is easy to think that, because you have used the spelling tool in Word for Windows, your work is accurate. Automatic spelling checks are very useful and you should always use them if they are available on your system, before you save or print a document but you must also proofread the document yourself. ~~Word's spelling facility compares each word you have keyed in with its own 'dictionary' of words.~~ //Candidates who fail examinations often do so because their proofreading is not adequate. One of the most common errors is the omission of words. Unfortunately, if you have missed out some words, or not deleted some words as instructed, spellchecking will not detect this.

[If you have typed the wrong 'version' of a word, eg (there) instead of (their), spelling check will not detect this as both versions are spelt correctly. However, Word's grammar tool should detect the error and suggest the correct version to you. //Only you can tell if you have copied names of people or places correctly and if a piece of information which you were asked to find is accurate. For example, spellcheck cannot tell if the date you have keyed in for 'Thursday of next week' is the correct one. Don't guess - use a diary or calendar. To check up on today's date, you could use Word's Date and Time facility which is found under the Insert Menu. (The current time is displayed on the Status Bar at the bottom of the screen.)

The skills of proofreading are essential in text processing. You should train yourself to check every detail in any work you have done before you print it so as not to waste paper. It is not enough to check the work on your screen, you must compare it with the 'copy' from which you are working - going through it word by word.

Typescript containing spelling errors

It is part of the text-processing operator's job to correct all spelling errors in the work being done. This task is made much easier by the use of the spelling tool. If you suspect while keying in that a word is spelt incorrectly, you can check it instantly by selecting the word and then using Word's spelling tool. You should also use the spelling tool when you have finished keying in the document so that any typographical errors are picked up and corrected before printing.

Exercise 1B

1.6 Starting a new file, key in the following document, correcting all the words which are incorrectly spelt:

Top Jobs Empoyment Agency

A new agency has placed an advertment in the local newspaper. Both tempory and permenent positions are processed by the agency and they announce that they have sufficent experence and contacts to accomodate requests from a wide range of buisnesses and clients.

A collegue of mine recommended the agency to us. She acheived her gaol of getting a responsable job dealing with comittee work and coresponding with foreign companys in the finacial field.   If you are looking for a new post, you could save some expence and incovenience though the use of an agency.

Althrough a fee is charged for the servise, you will receive acces to a range of jobs and there will be an oppertunity to discus your pervious learning and achievments with experienced staff who appreciate your skils and knowledge and who will take definate steps to develop your curiculum vitea and help you to prepare for an interview.   The agency staff may be able to recomend a career move or a coarse of learning which may not have been apparant to you. Most agencys have plenty of openings for:

WP Operaters
Book-keeping/acounts clarks
Personel Asistants/Senior Secretries
Adminstrators at all levells.

1.7 Use the spelling and grammar tools to check your work, and proof-read it yourself carefully.

1.8 Save your document, using filename **EX1B**. You do not need to print at this stage.

 ## Typescript containing correction signs

A word-processor operator is seldom given work which simply requires to be copied exactly as it is. A photocopier could do the job much more quickly! Usually, the 'copy' (text which the operator copies from) contains amendments.

Examples

amended

This sentence has been changed.

should be keyed in as **This sentence has been amended**.

Please delete or omit this word.

should be keyed in as **Please delete this word**.

this sentence

Extra words should be inserted for to make sense.

should be keyed in as **Extra words should be inserted for this sentence to make sense**.

You may be asked to move words or sentences or phrases.

should be keyed in as **You may be asked to move sentences or words or phrases**.

Start a new paragraph where you see either of these signs. The letters NP (new paragraph) may also appear in the margin.

// or [

Join two paragraphs together when the 'run on' sign is used.

To join two paragraphs, move the pointer to the first character of the second paragraph and press the backspace delete key twice.

Insert the word with the dotted line underneath it when you see a tick inside a circle (or the word *stet*) in the margin.

delete

(✓) When you type this sentence, insert this word.

should be typed as **When you type this sentence, insert this word**.

Transpose words or phrases when you see the transposition sign.

word1 word2

Two words in sentence this are the wrong way round.

should be typed as **Two words in this sentence are the wrong way round**.

Transpose text vertically when you see arrows like this. All words between the arrows should be moved.

Dot Matrix	LS345	*Should be typed as*:	Dot Matrix	DM223
Laser	DM223		Laser	LS345
Ink Jet	IJ555		Bubble Jet	BJ457
Bubble Jet	BJ457		Ink Jet	IJ555

Exercise 1C

1.9 Open the document you saved as EX1B if it is not already on screen. Amend the text as shown below. Use a ragged (unjustified) right margin.

Top Jobs Employment Agency ← *embolden and underline heading*

A new ~~employment~~ agency has placed an advertisement in the local *evening* newspaper. Both temporary and permanent positions are processed by the agency and they announce that they have sufficient experience and contacts to accommodate requests from a wide range of businesses and clients.

A colleague of mine recommended the agency ~~to us~~. She achieved her ~~goal~~ *aim* of getting a responsible job dealing with committee work and corresponding with foreign companies in the financial field. If you are looking for a new post, you could save some expense and inconvenience through the use of an agency.

☑ Although a fee is ~~charged~~ *levied* for the service, you will receive access to a range of jobs and there will be an opportunity to discuss your previous learning and achievements with experienced staff who appreciate your skills and ~~knowledge and~~ who will take definite steps to develop your curriculum vitae and help you to prepare for an interview. The agency staff may be able to recommend a career move or a course of learning which may not have been ~~apparent~~ *obvious* to you. Most agencies have plenty ☑ of ~~openings~~ *vacancies* for: (at present)

→ WP Operators
Book-keeping/accounts clerks.
Personal Assistants/Senior Secretaries
Administrators at all levels,

1.10 Use the spelling and grammar tools to check your work, and proof-read it yourself carefully.

1.11 Save and print your document, using filename **EX1C**. Check your print-out with that at the back of the book. If you find any errors, correct them and print again if necessary. Close the file.

i Copy containing abbreviations

Text authors often use abbreviations when writing out copy which is to be processed by a word-processor operator. In the work situation, you would quickly get used to individual authors' 'shorthand'.

The following list shows some abbreviations you can expect to come across in intermediate examinations:

accom	accommodation	dr	dear
a/c(s)	accounts	ex	exercise
ack	acknowledge	exp(s)	expense(s)
advert(s)	advertisement(s)	exp	experience
altho'	although	f/t	full time
approx	approximate(ly)	gntee(s)	guarantee(s)
appt(s)	appointment(s)	gov(s)	government(s)
bel	believe	immed	immediate(ly)
bus	business	incon	inconvenient(ence)
cat(s)	catalogue(s)	info	information
cttee(s)	committee(s)	mfr(s)	manufacturer(s)
co(s)	company/ies	misc	miscellaneous
def	definitely	necy	necessary

opp(s)	opportunity(ies)	thro'	through
org	organization	wd	would
p/t	part time	w	with
poss	possible	wh	which
rec	receive	wl	will
recd	received	yr(s)	years
recom	recommend	yr(s)	yours
ref(s)	reference(s)		
refd	referred		
resp	responsible	*Days of the week, e.g.:*	
sec(s)	secretary/ies	Wed	Wednesday
sep	separate		
sh	shall	*Months of the year, e.g.:*	
shd	should	Feb	February
sig(s)	signature(s)		
suff	sufficient	*Words in addresses, e.g.:*	
temp	temporary	Cres	Crescent

Complimentary closes, e.g.:
Yrs ffly   Yours faithfully
Yrs scly   Yours sincerely

At intermediate and advanced examination levels, abbreviations are not followed by a full stop. You are expected to recognize abbreviations and expand them correctly and consistently.

It is usual practice to retain other commonly used abbreviations such as **etc., eg, NB, &** (in company names but not in continuous text).

You may use a dictionary and the spelling tool in examinations.

Exercise 1D

1.12 Starting a new file, key in the following document, expanding all the abbreviations as you go along. Use a justified right margin.

Creating a good impression   (don't omit yr sig)

When you apply for a new job, you wl probably be requested todoso in the form of a letter of application or by completing an application form, & some cos also require a CV. After reading the advert, if you bel yr exp is suff and you wd like to work within the bus, you

NP shd make a def plan immed. [The presentation & content of yr letter and/or CV shd be effective enough to gntee an interview and therefore an opp. to give a good a/c of yourself. Don't forget to ✓ ask permission from referees to include there name in the refs section of yr CV or application form. Altho' most businesses ack receipt of all applications thro' the post (in a sep. letter), unfortunately some do not.

✓ If it is necy for you to travel some distance to an interview, the org wd normally refund yr travel exps & overnight accom costs.

This is a useful ex wh forces you to assess yr currant position and poss action you cd take to develop yr career.

Gather as much info as poss w ref to the bus or org thro' trade cats & mfr's literature, and make sure that you do not incon anyone by arriving late. (for yr appt)

Some people recom a trial run by train or bus in order to so that you wl be able to estimate the approx travelling time & become familiar w the route.   (Please put CV in full throughout)

1.13 Use the spelling and grammar tools to check your work, and proof-read it yourself carefully.

1.14 Save and print your document, using filename **EX1D**. Check your print-out with that at the back of the book. If you find any errors, correct them and print again if necessary. Close the file.

 ## Changing line length by adjusting left and right margins

In Word for Windows you can change the format of a document by increasing or decreasing the margins. You can use this facility to change the margins for the whole of a document or for certain sections only.

> Insetting the margins (or changing the line length) is often used to draw the reader's attention to a particular piece of information – like this!

If you use the mouse/ruler method you can see the margin markers move on screen. Use the ruler and the default tabs (every ½ inch) as a guide (e.g. to set a line length of 5 inches, you could position the left margin marker at 1 inch on the ruler and the right margin marker at 6 inches on the ruler).

Using this method, you can change margins:

- before keying in
- after keying in
- for a section of text only

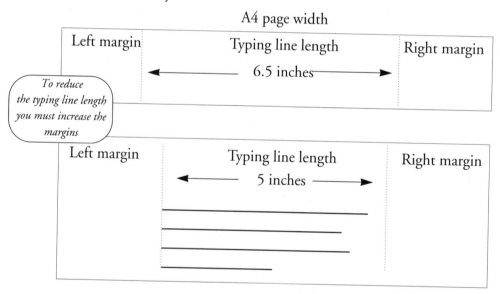

The left and right margins are usually preset at 1.25 inches or 3.17 cm. You may be given instructions to use margins in inches or in centimetres (or in both). If you change the units of measurement and make these the default settings, you can be sure of being accurate and you will not have to carry out a conversion. The unit you choose (inches or centimetres) will then be used in all relevant dialogue boxes.

Note: You may come across an instruction to change margins by, for example, 5 characters. This measurement relates to word-processing programs using 10-pitch (10 characters = 1 inch). In Word for Windows, use *inches*, i.e. ½ inch.

Change the units of measurement

To change to inches:
- Select: **Tools Options General**
- In the **Measurement Units** box select: **Inches**

To change to centimetres:
Follow instructions as above, selecting **Centimetres** in the **Measurement Units** drop-down menu

Margins

To set margins before keying in:

Mouse/menu bar

Specify page setup:

Select: **File Page Setup Margins**

In **Left** box key in: Measurement required (or use spin box)

Repeat in **Right** box if necessary

In the **Apply To** box, select: **Whole document**

Click on **OK** to operate changed margins for this document only

or

Click on **Default** to adopt these margins as the settings for the **Normal** template

Mouse/ruler markers

Display ruler on document screen:

Select: **View Ruler** (ruler is displayed at top of document screen)

Display tabs on ruler line:

Select: **Format Tabs**

Check following settings: **Default Tab** stops – 0.5 inch; **Alignment** – Left; **Leader** – None

You can display the tab stops more clearly by clicking on the tab-stop marker: ⬛ is displayed.

To change the left margin:

Click and drag the small rectangle at the left of the ruler line ⬗ to the position required

To change the right margin:

Click and drag the small triangle at the right of the ruler line ◮ to the position required

To change margins in an existing document:

Keyboard/mouse

Select the document (**Ctrl + A**) and then operate any of the commands shown above

To change margins for a section of a document:

Keyboard/mouse

Select the text (as previously described) and then operate the commands shown above

Exercise 1E

1.15 Change the unit of measurement currently being used to **inches**.

1.16 Open the document you saved as EX1C. Make the following changes to the format of the document:

- justified right margin
- line length of 5½ inches (14 cm)
- double-line spacing for first paragraph

1.17 Save your document using filename **EX1E** and print preview. Compare your document with the print-out check at the back of the book and, if the format is not correct, reread the instructions and amend the format if necessary. Close the file.

1.18 Open the document you saved as EX1D. Make the following changes to the format of the document:

- ragged right margin
- line length of 5 inches (13 cm)
- double-line spacing for last paragraph

1.19 Save your document using filename **EX1F** and print preview. Compare your document with the print-out check at the back of the book and, if the format is not correct, reread the instructions and amend the format if necessary. Close the file.

1.20 Exit the program or continue straight on to the next unit.

UNIT 2 Business documents

At the end of Unit 2 you will have learnt how to
- *prepare business letters and memorandums with continuation sheets*
- *print letters on preprinted letterheads*
- *insert page breaks*
- *insert page numbering*
- *locate information in another document and insert in current document*
- *identify and correct inconsistencies in text*
- *indicate routeing of copies on business documents*

 ## Business letter layout: reminders

You should have already learnt how to set out a business letter as part of your elementary text-processing training. A business letter is written on behalf of an organization and is printed or typed on the organization's own letterhead, which gives all relevant details such as address, telephone and fax numbers.

In intermediate examinations, you may be asked to produce a business letter on plain paper or on a preprinted letterhead. Use the following format:

- Block everything at the left-hand margin – do not indent paragraphs or centre items.
- Date the letter with today's date – use automatic date-insertion facility to save time.
- Use open punctuation – no punctuation except in the body of the letter.
- Leave at least one clear line space between the different parts of the letter, and between paragraphs.
- If the salutation is formal, e.g. 'Dear Sir or Madam', finish your letter with the complimentary close: 'Yours faithfully'.
- If the salutation is informal, e.g. 'Dear Mrs Smith', finish your letter with the complimentary close: 'Yours sincerely'.
- Leave several clear lines for the person sending the letter to write his or her signature.
- Special marks such as CONFIDENTIAL, PRIVATE, PERSONAL, URGENT, FOR THE ATTENTION OF, etc., should be given some form of emphasis such as bold, underlining or capitalization. (The special mark should also be inserted on the envelope.)
- The enclosure mark is usually placed at the end of a letter with one clear line space above and below it.

Consistency of presentation

Measurements, weights, times, money

You should always be consistent in the way you present information within a document. The following are examples of points you should watch out for.

Be consistent in the use of an abbreviation to represent a *measurement* or *weight,* such as **mm, cm, ft, in, kg, oz, lb**. For example, don't key in **30"** in one place and **24 in** somewhere else in the document. Be consistent – use either **"** or **in** but not a mixture of the two.

You may leave one space before the abbreviation or no spaces but you must be consistent. For example, don't key in **46kg** in one place and **46 kg** somewhere else in the document.

Stick to the 12-hour clock or the 24-hour clock when using *times.* For example, don't key in **1600 hrs** in one place and **7.30 am** somewhere else in the document. Be consistent in the use of **pm, o'clock, hrs**.

When using an abbreviation for *currency* (e.g. **$, £, DM, F**), stick to one method of presentation. For example, don't key in **£15** in one place and **£12.50** somewhere else in the document. Both amounts should show the pence – **£15.00** and **£12.50**. Don't key in **FF100** in one place and **100 French francs** somewhere else in the document. You should use either **£** or **p** but not both together in one amount – **£0.50p** is wrong.

Words and figures

Be consistent in the way you present *numbers* within a document. For example, don't key in **40 miles** in one place and **fifty-five miles** somewhere else in the document. Look through the text first and decide on words or figures. Think about these two examples:

- **1,234,650** is difficult to express in words
- **1** looks strange as the first word of a sentence.

Other possible inconsistencies

Be consistent in using the *dash* (–) or the *hyphen* (-) between words and symbols. The keyboard symbol is the same, the spacing either side of the symbol is different. (A dash 'separates' words and has one space before and after. A hyphen 'joins' words and has no spaces before and after.) Don't key in **4 to 6** in one place and **16-21** somewhere else in the document. The word **to** can also be used in **3 to 4 weeks' time, Tuesday to Thursday**. Don't key in **Friday – Sunday** in one place and **Monday to Wednesday** somewhere else in the document.

Be consistent in the presentation of *per cent.* For example, don't key in **50%** in one place and **100 per cent** somewhere else in the document.

When keying in words which can be *spelt in two different ways,* make sure all occurrences match. For example, don't key in **organise** in one place and **organize** somewhere else in the document.

Be consistent in the amount of space you leave after *punctuation.* For example, don't leave **1 space** after a full stop in one place and **2 spaces** after a full stop somewhere else in the document.

You should standardize the *layout* of any document which you are producing. For example, don't mix paragraph styles (e.g. keep them all blocked to the left or all indented) and make all headings the same style (e.g. all in capitals or all in lower case and underlined).

Locating information in another document

As part of intermediate examinations you will be asked to insert information into a document which can be found in another document. (At work, you would be expected to consult paper files, computer databases, etc.) Take notice of the text you are keying in so that you will be able to select the correct piece of information to make your document accurate.

Exercise 2A

2.1 Key in the following letter using a justified right margin:.

Ref ADEX/SB (Mark letter urgent please) (Line length 5¾")

Mr Martin Wise
I J E ___ Agency ← (Please obtain name of agency from EXIC)
Occupation House
South Pl
DARLINGTON   DN3 5ON

Dr Mr W___ ← (Subject heading - ADVERTISING LITERATURE)

Further to our recent conversation at the ADEX show, I have pleasure in enclosing our cat wh gives full info on our wide range of (services). [Our org has invested in the latest (technology) in order to realise the highest quality work and this investment has paid off – a 25% increase in bus over the (passed) 6 months and etc a predicted rise of over 30 per cent in the coming twelve months.

The 'Hi-flyers' range wh I mentioned as a poss solution to yr co are available in two sizes – A4 (210mm by 297 mm) and A5 (149 mm × 210mm). Paper used may be 80gsm or 100 gsm.

Costs (ranges) from £25.50 to £50 per thousand, depending on the quality, (size and complexity) of the art [work.]

If colour printing is requested, the price wd start at ~~around~~ about ✓ ~~thirty-five~~ ~~fifteen~~ pounds. This is merely an approx guide and we can discuss (financail) details when we meet.

I realize that it is necy for us to get together asap so I have asked my sec – Maria Calder – to ring you to arrange a def appt for me to visit your office w our presentation portfolio. I cd be w you between 9.30 am and 1630 hrs from Mon to Wed; from Thurs – Sat I am based at the Sunderland office. I hope to see you in the near future.

Yrs sncly

Susanne Beaumont

2.2   Save and print your document using filename **EX2A**. Check your print-out with that at the back of the book. If you find any errors, correct them and print again if necessary.

 ## Memorandum layout: reminders

You will have already learnt how to set out a memorandum as part of your elementary text-processing training. A memorandum is sent from one department or branch of an organization to another and is printed or typed on the organization's own memo form, which gives all relevant details such as name of sender, name of recipient, date, reference and subject. The telephone and fax numbers of the department sending the memo may also be included.

In intermediate examinations you may be asked to produce a memorandum on plain paper (keying in all the headings) or using a template (inserting information against stored headings). Use the following format:

*   Block everything at the left-hand margin – do not indent paragraphs or centre items.

*   Date the memo with today's date – use automatic date-insertion facility to save time.

*   Use open punctuation – no punctuation except in the body of the memo.

*   Leave at least one clear line space between the different parts of the memo, and between paragraphs.

*   Special marks such as CONFIDENTIAL, PRIVATE, PERSONAL, URGENT, FOR THE ATTENTION OF, etc., should be given some form of emphasis such as bold, underlining or capitalization.

*   The enclosure mark is usually placed at the end of a memo with at least one clear line space above and below it.

*   Memos do not contain a salutation or complimentary close, although the author may initial it.

Exercise 2B

2.3   Key in the memo template shown on the *left* below, emboldening all headings and aligning at the left margin as shown:

MEMORANDUM	**MEMORANDUM**	
To:	**To:**	All WP Students
From:	**From:**	WP Tutor
Ref:	**Ref:**	Memo/Unit2
Date:	**Date:**	(Today's date)

Align text at tab stop when completing memo form, as shown here

2.4 Save your document using filename **MEMOFORM**. Close the file.

Routeing of copies

It is normal practice for the sender to keep one copy of a letter or memo for reference. Additional copies may be required for other people and this is indicated at the foot of the document.

Instructions may be given as follows:

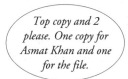

Top copy and 2 please. One copy for Asmat Khan and one for the file.

The routeing indication is inserted at the bottom of the document (under any enclosure indication), e.g.:

Copy: **Asmat Khan**

File

When all the copies of the document have been printed, it is normal practice to indicate the destination of each copy by ticking (or underlining in coloured pen or using a highlighting pen).

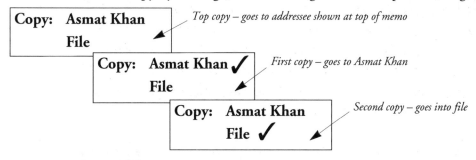

Top copy – goes to addressee shown at top of memo

First copy – goes to Asmat Khan

Second copy – goes into file

Exercise 2C	**2.5** Open the file MEMOFORM to display your memo template on screen.
	2.6 Key in the memo on the following page, inserting the information against the headings. Align the inserted text at the first available tab stop as shown previously. Use a ragged right margin.
	2.7 Save and print your document using filename **EX2C.** Check your printout with that at the back of the book. If you find any errors, correct them and print again if necessary.

Memo to Flora Sim, Training Officer from Edward Dent, Health & Safety Officer

Ref ED/HS/Training

(line length 5" please)

(Mark memo CONFIDENTIAL)

(CAPS) Health and Safety Training (European)

Recent (directives (has) highlighted areas of concern ✓ for (medium) (and) (small)-sized cos, and I was asked to organize a thorough (survay) of the whole org to identify any problems areas. /Although employees may must be consulted and (there) proposals shd be considered, it is the (employers') absolute overall responsibility to avoid, evaluate & combat all risks.

✓ (Work (systems) (and) (conditions) must be adapted to suit individual and group needs. Occupations involving specific (hazzards) must have those hazards clearly identified and explained to employees, and employers are obliged to ensure that any (measures (recommended) are implemented immed.

The (mane) risks have been identified and evaluated and, in the majority of cases, only minor changes improvements are necy. If you are interested, I wd be pleased to explain my findings and discuss these w you. [The H___ & S___ Action Plan is to be circulated within the next few weeks days. Training features will, of course, be a form a large part of the plan and I wd like to organise the implementation of this w you. [I wl be on holiday until Mon (give date & 1st Mon of next month). Please telephone me on my return.

_i_ Documents with continuation sheet

In intermediate examinations you will be asked to prepare documents which will take up more than one sheet of A4 paper. You will be required to insert page breaks (new page markers) in an appropriate place and to set automatic page numbering so that all subsequent pages are numbered.

Page breaks in business documents

Page breaks should be inserted in sensible places within a document so that it is easy to read. Word will show a 'soft' page break (a horizontal dotted line) on screen when the maximum number of lines has been used. The printer will start a new page at this point.

A 'hard' page break is inserted by the operator and is displayed as a horizontal dotted line with the words '**Page Break**' in the centre of the line. You should get into the habit of inserting hard page breaks after all other text formatting and amendments have been carried out and just before printing.

Consider the following points when paginating (inserting page breaks in) a multi-page document:

- The complimentary close of a letter (Yours…) should never be the *only* text on the last page. Ideally, there should be at least three or four lines of text above the complimentary close.
- You should not divide a word between one page and the next.
- You should not leave only the first line of a paragraph at the bottom of a page (a 'widow').
- You should not carry forward only the last line of a paragraph on to the next page (an 'orphan').

Insert a new page break

When keying in a long document, Word automatically inserts 'soft' page breaks for you. You can insert a 'hard' page break whenever you want to start a new page – e.g. the start of a new chapter.

Keyboard	Mouse and menu
Position insertion pointer where you want to insert the page break:	
Press: **Ctrl + ↵** (return)	Select: **Insert, Break, Page Break, OK**

Widow/orphan control

Word allows you automatically to avoid widows and orphans. Check that your program is defaulted to this option:

Mouse and menu

Select: **Format, Paragraph, Text Flow**

Check that widow/orphan box is displayed as follows:
All other boxes should be blank

Pagination
[X] Widow/Orphan Control

Page numbering (insert method)

The pages of a multi-page document should all be numbered. Word allows you to set the page numbering once – page numbers will then appear automatically on all pages.

Keyboard	Mouse and menu
Move pointer to required position Press: **Alt + Shift + P** (page number appears on screen)	Select: **Insert, Page Numbers**

The **Page Numbers** dialogue box is displayed on screen:

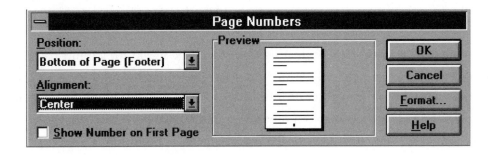

- Page numbering offers choice of **Position, Alignment, Show Number on First Page**
- The **Preview** box shows the page number in position

Select from the page numbers dialogue box as appropriate:

Button	Action
Position	Select position on page *vertically* – bottom or top
Alignment	Select position on page *horizontally* – left, right, centre (**Inside** and **Outside** are used with binding margins)
Show Number on First Page	Remove **X** to omit number on first page (if required on letters)
Preview	Displays page number in position chosen
Format	Allows format of page number to be selected, i.e. Arabic, roman, letters

Note: Page numbers show on screen in page layout view and Print Preview only.

Printing on letterhead

In Word the top margin is usually set by default to 1 inch. When printing on a letterhead, the top margin *on the first page only* should be increased to accommodate the printed heading. (Second and subsequent pages are printed on plain paper.)

You may need to measure the depth of the letterheaded paper you intend to use, and to experiment to find the top margin measurement required. Find out how to insert letterheaded paper into the paper feed tray of your printer so that the document is printed in the correct position.

Change the top margin for letterheaded paper:

Mouse and menu

Key in the whole document before carrying out this procedure

Position the pointer immediately before the first letter of the document:

Select: **Format, Paragraph**

Key in: Required measurement in **Spacing, Before** box (you may use any unit of measurement – e.g. 1 inch or 2 cm or 25 mm); click on **OK**

Word's default top margin is 1 inch. To leave a 2 inch top margin, key in 1 inch in the **Before** box. This will add 1 inch to the existing default margin of 1 inch.

Note: The above setting will be changed to a point size measurement and will remain selected until it is changed or deleted.

Exercise 2D

2.8 Open the document you saved as EX2A and add the following text as instructed below. Change the right margin to ragged format.

You expressed interest in our 'Infolda ~~Infolda~~

> Top + 2 please. Copies to Adam R and to file

'Infofolda' product wh can (accomodate) approx 15 to twenty pages (usually suff for most cos' needs). Covers are laminated and may include a stud fastening system or elasticated cross bands. Many agencies & mfrs recom this folder and we bel the (initial) ~~o/p~~ is justified. The materials contained in the folder can be replaced when necy w the latest up-to-date info. The folder itself does not need to be issued every time services, prices or other details are ~~amended~~ changed. You can simply forward the sep sheets of info thro' the post w a covering letter.

You may recall that my (colleage), Adam Randall, wished to be kept informed of our plans, so I ~~will~~ have sent a copy of this letter to him at our Head Office.

Adam has recently been appointed to Head of Marketing and he is particularly (interested) in our involvement in exhibitions ~~like~~ such as ~~the~~ ADEX Show.

> Please insert above as 5th para onwards, ie after the para about costs and colour printing

---

2.9 Change the top margin on the first page to 2 inches so that you can print on a letterhead.

2.10 Your document will take up more than one page – you should see that a 'soft page break' has appeared in your document. Insert a 'hard page break' in a suitable place.

2.11 Insert page numbering at top left so that the second page is numbered but not the first one.

2.12 Print preview the letter to check that the top margin, page break and page numbering are correct. If not, make the necessary adjustments.

2.13 Save your document using filename **EX2D.** Print your document on plain A4 paper.

2.14 Using one of the letterheads included in this book and the print-out you have just produced, check to make sure that the top margin on the first page is deep enough to accommodate the printed head. If not, adjust the top margin as necessary.

2.15 Compare your print-out with that at the back of the book. If you find any errors in the text, correct them now.

2.16 Save and print three copies of the letter (EX2D), using letterheaded paper for the first page and plain paper for the second page. Mark the copies to indicate the routeing of each copy, using a tick, underline or highlighting pen.

NB If you have used a header to insert your name, you may find that this disappears on the first page if you suppress the page numbering.

Insert this text just ~~before~~ last paragraph – I wl be on holiday...

My preliminary ideas are given below:

Training is needed in the following ~~topics~~ areas : ← embolden this line

1 Purchase of new machinery
2 Evaluation of existing equipment – standards & function
3 Work areas and work stations,
4 Manual (operations/handling) – 1929 regulations
5 Display screen equipment
6 D___ S___ operation – legal aspects
7 Personal protection – physical, biological & chemical risks
8 Equipment and machine operation
9 Fire extinguishers & evacuation procedures
10 Signs & warnings
11 First Aid   12 Hygiene   in full
~~12~~ 13 Handicapped workers

I anticipate that all members of staff shd rec training in items three, four, seven, nine, ten & thirteen above. In addition, Admin staff shd rec training in items 5 and 6. Catering staff shd rec additional training in items eight & 12. Production staff wl probably need extra training in items 2 and 8. External training wl be provided for first-aiders. I wd suggest that the initial phase of training shd run between Jan – Feb, and shd cover item 3 (W_A_ and w_), item 7 (P_ p_ etc) and item 10 (Fire ext_ etc) because the safety of personel is paramount.

                          rest
☑ The ~~remainder~~ of the training programme cd probably be delivered between Mar – May. All training is to be carried out at the co's exp and during working hours.

I enclose a copy of a proposed timetable for training. Obviously, we need to discuss this in more detail. I have sent a copy of this memo to the Personnel Officer for info.

Please indicate routeing:
– Personnel O—
– Training file

2.18 Your document will take up more than one page. Insert a 'hard page break' in a suitable place.

2.19 Insert page numbering at bottom centre so that the second page is numbered but not the first one.

2.20 Print preview the memo to check that the page break and page numbering are correct. If not, make the necessary adjustments.

2.21 Save and print one copy of your document using filename **EX2E.** Compare your print-out with that at the back of the book. If you find any errors in the text, correct them now.

2.22 Save and print three copies of the memo. Mark the copies to indicate the routeing of each copy, using a tick, underline or highlighting pen.

2.23 Exit the program if you have finished working or continue straight on to the next unit.

3 *Multi-page documents*

At the end of Unit 3 you will have learnt how to
- *insert headers and footers*
- *change the format of a multi-page document in the following ways:*
  - *paginate as requested*
  - *change line spacing as requested*
  - *allocate space*
  - *rearrange text by moving and copying blocks*
  - *search and replace text throughout a document*

i Headers and footers

A *header* is a piece of text in the form of a title, heading or reference which appears at the top of all pages of a multi-page document. A *footer* is the same kind of text appearing at the bottom of all pages. Headers and footers are printed within the top and bottom margins.

This word-processing function allows you to 'set' the headers and footers by keying in the text once only. The header or footer will then automatically appear on all pages. Headers and footers can be edited if the text or layout needs to be changed.

Using the header/footer function in intermediate examinations

In intermediate examinations, you will be asked to insert a header or a footer in a two- or three-page document, and also to insert page numbering on second and subsequent pages (omitting the page number on page 1 of letters). Unfortunately, it is not possible in Word to omit the page number on the first page *and* use a header/footer because page numbering operates within the header/footer text box and a request for the first page to be different (i.e. not numbered) prompts Word to expect the header/footer also to be different on the first page.

This means that you will have to key in the header twice – once on the first page and again on the second page. Although the benefit of using a header and footer in this way may not be apparent in a two-page document, if you were producing a document with many pages, the value of the header/footer command would be obvious. You should practise using headers/footers so that you are familiar with the concept and you could use them in employment and in any other work.

Tip: If you find that headers and footers are not present in Print Preview, it may be necessary to increase the header/footer space allowance by changing the page setup as follows:

Select: **File, Page Setup**

Increase: The measurement in the **From Edge** box (**Header** or **Footer** as appropriate)

Headers and footers

Set the format for headers and footers:

*   Before keying in
*   After keying in

Mouse and menu

Position the insertion pointer at the beginning of the document:

Select: <u>V</u>iew, <u>H</u>eader and Footer

The **Header** text box and the **Header and Footer** Tool Bar are displayed on screen:

To insert a text header:

Key in the required text in the header text box (header and footer text can be formatted in the same way as document text – e.g. tab stops, text emphasis, font changes)

Click on **OK**

To insert a text footer:

Click on the ⊞ **Switch between Header and Footer** button on the Header and Footer Tool Bar

Key in the required text in the footer text box

Click on **OK**

The following options are available on the Header and Footer Tool Bar:

Tool Tip title	Function
Show Previous **Show Next** **Same as Previous**	Used when creating headers and footers differently for even/odd pages
Page Numbers **Date** **Time**	Automatically insert current details into a header or footer
Page Setup	Displays Page Setup dialogue box – to allow changes to margins, layout, etc.
Show/Hide Document Text	Shows or hides current document on screen – a toggle switch
Close	Closes Header and Footer Tool Bar and returns to document screen

Note: Headers and footers show on screen in page layout view and Print Preview only.

Deleting headers, footers and page numbering:

Mouse and menu

Select: **View, Header and Footer**

Select: Header text, footer text or page number using mouse

Press: ← (backspace key) or **Del(ete)**

Use **Print Preview** or **Page Layout View** to check deletion

Exercise 3A

3.1 Open the file saved as **EX2E** and delete the page numbering.
Set a *header* to show the following details:

Your name   Exercise 3A   Centre No (if applicable)

If you have already typed these details at the top of the exercise, delete them from the document – otherwise they will be printed twice!

3.2 Check that the header is present on both pages of the document by selecting **Page Layout View** or by selecting **File, Print Preview**.

3.3 Save and print your document using filename **EX3A.** Close the file.

Exercise 3B

3.4 Open the file saved as **EX2D** and delete the page numbering.
Set a *footer* to show the following details:

Your name   Exercise 3B   Centre No (if applicable)

If you have already typed these details at the top of the exercise, delete them from the document – otherwise they will be printed twice!

3.5 Check that the footer is present on both pages of the document by selecting **Page Layout View** or by selecting **File, Print Preview**.

3.6 Save and print your document (on plain paper or on letterhead) using filename **EX3B.** Close the file.

Page numbering (header and footer method)

You have already used the *Insert* method of page numbering. This is the best method of page numbering as you have more control over format, position, etc. However, there is an alternative method – to use the header and footer command which you have just practised.

Mouse and menu

Select: **View, Header and Footer**

The **Header** text box and the **Header and Footer** Tool Bar are displayed on screen:

Header

Header and Footer
Close

To insert page numbering as a header:

Click on: [#] **Page Numbers** button on **Headers and Footers** Tool Bar

Current page number appears in the header text box; change alignment to centre or right if required

Click on: **Close**

To insert page numbering as a footer:

Click on: [⊞] **Switch between Header and Footer** button on Tool Bar

Click on: [#] **Page Numbers** button on **Headers and Footers** Tool Bar

Current page number appears in the footer text box; change alignment to centre or right if required

Click on: **Close**

Note: Page numbers show on screen in Page Layout View and Print Preview only.

 ## Multi-page documents: formatting requirements

In intermediate examinations, you will be expected to make the following formatting changes to multi-page documents.

Allocating space (e.g. for photographs)

To leave a given number of *clear lines*, press ↵ (return) once for each clear line required and once more, e.g. to leave 6 clear lines, press ↵ 7 times starting on the same line and at the end of the previous text.

To leave a given measurement in *inches, mm, cm, points,* use the **Format, Paragraph** command, keying in the measurement required (in the stated unit of measurement) in the **Before** box.

Insetting margins (changing line length/margins settings) for a section of text or for a whole document

Use the **View, Ruler** command. Select text and then move left and/or right margin markers along the horizontal ruler to the appropriate position using the mouse.

Indenting text

Use the [⊟] **Decrease Indent** [⊟] **Increase Indent** buttons on the Formatting Tool Bar or the **Shortcut** keys as follows:

Ctrl + M to indent a paragraph at the left (**Ctrl + Q** to remove the indent)

Ctrl + T to indent enumerated paragraphs (**Ctrl + Q** to remove the indent)

Moving and copying blocks of text

Read the instructions carefully – don't confuse the terms 'move' and 'copy':

Move a block means that the text appears in one place only – you simply have to reposition the block.

Copy a block means that the text appears in two (or more) places – you leave the block in its original position *and* put an identical copy of it in another position.

Leaving clear line spaces between separate parts of a document

You should leave at least one clear line space in the following situations:

- between paragraphs and separate parts of a document
- before and after headings
- between listed items (if instructed to do so in the task)

 ## Organizing text editing in a multi-page document

When a document runs into several pages and there are many changes to be made, you may sometimes feel that you have become 'lost' – particularly if you have been distracted. The following is a *suggested* method of working which you might like to adopt.

After setting headers and page numbering and viewing to check that they are correct:

1 Carry out all the necessary **text amendments**, e.g. inserting or deleting of text *throughout the whole document.*

2 **Move** blocks of text and **copy** blocks of text as requested *throughout the whole document.*

3 **Search and replace text** as requested.

4 **Allocate space** (clear lines or given measurement) and **indent** or **inset** margins as requested.

5 **Paginate** your document as requested or as you think fit (read the instructions).

6 **Spellcheck** the whole document (use the **grammar tool** as well if necessary).

7 **Proof-read** the whole document, comparing word for word with the copy.

8 **Print Preview** your document to make sure that it is going to be printed correctly.

9 And finally, **print** your work.

 ## Moving around the document quickly

When you are checking and proof-reading a multi-page document, you need to be able to move quickly from one section to another. Practise the following quick cursor movements so that you become familiar with them and use them regularly.

Moving around the text: quick methods

To move	Keyboard
Left word by word	Press: **Ctrl + ←** (arrow key) (hold down the **Ctrl** key and press the **←** key while the **Ctrl** key is still held down)
Right word by word	Press: **Ctrl + →**
To the end of the line	Press: **End**
To the start of the line	Press: **Home**
To top of paragraph	Press: **Ctrl + ↑**
To bottom of paragraph	Press: **Ctrl + ↓**
Up one screen	Press: **Page Up**
Down one screen	Press: **Page Down**
To the top of the document	Press: **Ctrl + Home**
To the bottom of the document	Press **Ctrl + End**

Go-to command:

Keyboard	**Mouse**
Press: **Ctrl + G**	Select: **Edit, Go To**

The **Go To** dialogue box is displayed on screen:

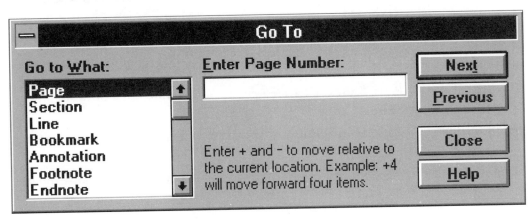

Select from the options available as appropriate:

Go to What:	Select: Type of location, e.g. page, line, field
Enter Page Number:	Key in page number required
	Note: to go forward 2 pages, key in **+2**
	to go back 4 pages, key in **-4**
Go To/Next	Moves to next occurrence displayed in **Go to What** box
Previous	Moves to previous occurrence of item displayed in **Go to What** box

 ### Deleting text quickly

When you are checking and proof-reading a multi-page document, you need to be able to delete blocks of text quickly. Practise the following quick-selection techniques so that you become familiar with them and use them regularly.

Selecting text

When you want to change a block of text in some way, it is necessary first of all to select or highlight the particular section of text. In Word for Windows this is called *selecting* text. The selected text shows in reverse – white letters on a black background, e.g. **Selected text**

To select	Keyboard	Mouse
One character (or more)	Press: **Shift + →** *or* **Shift + ←** (repeat until all required text is selected)	**Click and drag** mouse pointer across text
One word	Press: **Shift + Ctrl + →** *or* **Shift + Ctrl + ←**	**Double-click** on word
To the end of the line	Press: **Shift + End**	**Click and drag** mouse pointer right or down
To the beginning of the line	Press: **Shift + Home**	**Click and drag** mouse pointer left or up
A full line	Position pointer at beginning of line and press: **Shift + End** *or* Position pointer at end of line and press: **Shift + Home**	Position pointer in left margin (selection border) next to required line and **click**
A paragraph	—	Position pointer in selection border and **double-click** *or* Position pointer within paragraph and **triple-click**
The whole document	Press: **Ctrl + A**	Position pointer in selection border and **triple-click**
Any block of text	—	Position pointer at beginning of text, press: **Shift**. Then position pointer at end of text and **click**

To remove selection:

Click in any white space within document screen

Delete a block of text

- Select: Text to be deleted as previously described in 'Selecting text'
- Press: **Del(ete) Y(es)** *or* Press: **←** (backspace delete key)

Quick delete and insert text

To delete an incorrect section of text (of any size) and replace with correct text (of any size), simply select the incorrect text and key in the new text:

- Select: The text to be deleted as previously described in 'Selecting text'
- Without moving the insertion point, key in the new text

(The incorrect text which was initially selected will disappear.)

Exercise 3C

3.7 Starting a new file, key in the following document with the format shown below:

- Header (top left): **Your name   Exercise 3C   Centre No** (if relevant) (It will be necessary for you to key in the header on both pages!)

- Footer (bottom right): **TELEWORKING**

- Page numbering: **bottom left on second and subsequent pages**

- Right margin: **justified**

- Line spacing: **single except where instructed otherwise**

- Line length: **4½ inches**

(WORKING FROM HOME) — underline and centre

Research shows taht going to work causes stress and even illness. A healthy (buisness) needs
                                                                                          made
healthy staff but workers are actually being/ill by factors such as (trafic) chaos, accidents,

transport strikes and delays.

employment

The average worker spends two hours a day travelling to and from their job - an additional
         on top of
25% to working hours. In bad weather conditions, journeys can be long and very unpleasant
                                                                          increase
and the dramatically rising levels of pollution have lead to an enormous rise in the incidence
                            a
of (ashtma) The common cold, influenza and other virus infections spread rapidly in/stuffy
       environment
working conditions and poor (venitlation) can cause (headaches) (and) (sinus troubles).

A report by a management consultant cy for a group of bosses (suggest) that the solution is to

allow people to work from home - 'teleworking' is the term used to describe this. It has been
                                                                                  %
shown that (that) teleworkers take less time off sick and do an average of 45 per cent more

work.

       currently
The country/loses over 400 million working days through sickness per year.

(leave 1" here for diagram)

Approx 7 in ten bosses wl try teleworking before the end of the century as developments in
computers
information technology make links between home and office more and more (sophisitcated).

(START PG 2 HERE)   (E-mail)

Electronic mail is the key to (teleowkring) Documents can be written and transmitted without
                                                    sent
the use of paper. Messages can be transmitted at any time - locations and time zones do not

need to be taken into consideration as the communication is stored on the computer until the

'mailbox' is opened by the individual concerned

It is estimated that almost two million people are now working from home in Britain and they

spend more than fifty per cent of their time in doing so. They can go into the office after the

rush hour and at times to suit them.

Please put first 3 paras
in double line spacing

3.8 Print Preview your document to check that headers, footers, page numbering are correct. Spellcheck and proof-read your work.

3.9 Save and print your document using filename **EX3C**. Check your print-out with that at the back of the book. If you find any errors, correct them and print again if necessary.

Exercise 3D

3.10 Open the document **EX3C** if it is not already on screen. Add the following text to the end of the document:

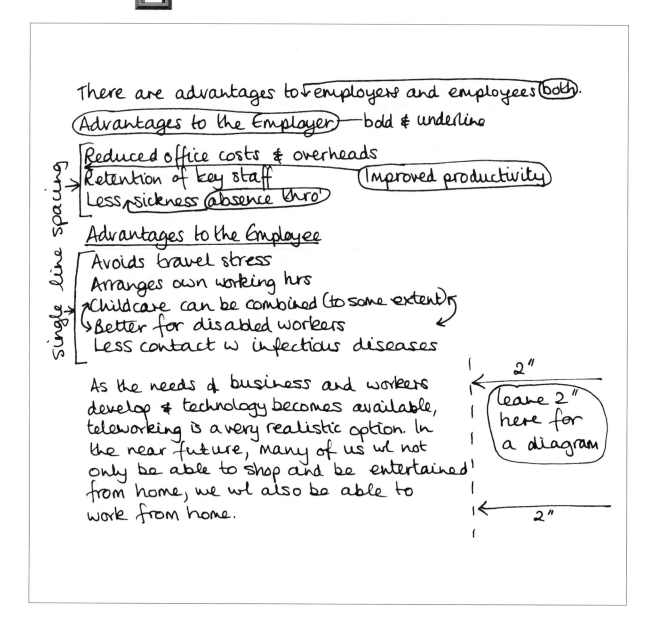

3.11 Save your file, using filename **EX3D.** Do not print at this stage.

Exercise 3E

3.12 Open the file **EX3D** if it is not already on screen. Make the following amendments to the document:

- Move the first paragraph to become the second paragraph
- Copy the heading **WORKING FROM HOME** to *just before the text added in Exercise 3D*
- Change the format of the items under both 'Advantages' sections to double-line spacing
- Leave a space of 1½ inches between the two 'Advantages' sections
- Replace **bosses** with **employers** throughout the document
- Amend the *header* to show **Exercise 3E**

3.13 Print Preview your document to check that your amendments are correct and complete. Spellcheck and proof-read your work.

3.14 Save and print your document using filename **EX3E.** Check your print-out with that at the back of the book. If you find any errors, correct them and print again if necessary.

Exercise 3F

3.15 Open the file **EX3E** if it is not already on screen. Make the following amendments:

- Change right margin to *ragged* format
- Change line length to *13cm (5 inches)* or *50 characters*
- Delete the footer **TELEWORKING**
- Insert a new footer to show **date and time**
- Amend the header to show **Exercise 3F** and also to include **TELEWORKING** after your name as follows:

```
 _ _ Header_ _ _ _ _ _ _ _ _ _ _ _ _ _ _
|
|  Your name   Exercise 3F   Centre No
|
|  TELEWORKING
|
|_ _ _ _ _ _ _ _ _ _ _ _ _ _ _ _ _ _ _ _ _ _ _ _ _
```

3.16 Print Preview your document to check that your amendments are correct and complete.

3.17 Save and print your document using filename **EX3F.** Check your print-out with that at the back of the book. If you find any errors, reread the instructions for formatting, correct them and print again if necessary.

3.18 Exit the program if you have finished working or continue straight on to the next unit.

Task 4A

Mark **Urgent** and print on a College Letterhead (Vine Tree)

Letterhead included in this book

Our ref (VCB/VF/accom2)

Ms Helen Forsyth
3A Maple Ave West
Chestnut Pk
ROYAL LEAMINGTON SPA
CV31 8PAT   (Warwickshire)

Dr Ms F_____

Thankyou for yr application for the Cordon Bleu Diploma ^course wh ~~is currently~~ wl be duly processed by our Admissions Tutor. [I am writing in response to yr letter in wh you requested info about the type of accom available to f/t students.]

(The College is situated just outside the old, walled City of York in an attractive, rural setting near to the (Ouse River). Students are housed in 2-storey ^blocks surrounding a central court(-)yard. Ample car/bike parking is provided adjacent to the accom blocks. //Each room is centrally-heated, fully-furnished and has an en(-)suite bathroom. Self-catering kitchens are shared by approx 6 students. ^An illustrated brochure is enclosed.

✓ (Accomodation) can be ~~booked~~ ^reserved by completing the enclosed form and returning it to me, preferably before the end of (last day of next month). You shd clearly state yr preference for a smoking/non-smoking, single/mixed-sex block.

Yrs sncly

Save as TASK4A

Veronique Flaubert
Accom Officer

Task 4B

Single line spacing except where shown

Number pages except first page

VINE TREE COLLEGE
CULINARY ARTS COURSES ← emphasise and ~~underline~~ centre

leave 2½" (63 mm) here for photo

The College offers residential accom in an attractive, rural setting just outside York. The
workrooms/are fully⊙fitted with the latest up-to-date specialist equipment.   *and the Training Restaurant*

Because of the practical nature of the courses, and the need for personal tuition and creative

developement, we have set a maximum number of 10 students on all programmes, including

the full/time Diploma.

double line spacing for these paras

CORDON BLEU DIPLOMA ← emphasise

A one-year f/t programme leading to the College's Diploma in Cordon Bleu Cookery.   ←

Assessment is continuous thoughout the yr and consists of practical and written assignments.

A final examination is taken in June.

The Diploma is a well-respected qualification throughout the country.

Successful students will be acredited with a nationally recognised qualification in Proffesional

Cookery.

Students will acquire a thoroguh grounding in basic principles and skills and then progress to

advanced culinary techniques. Former students have been successful in obtaining

employment in restraunts both in this country and abroad. Some students have continued

into higher education.

Justified Margins please

Task 4B cont

In addition to the food preparation module, students will gain knowledge and skills in spirits and wines, floral art, interior decor, business skills and food hygiene. A study tour in a European country (normally Belgium, France or Italy) are an optional part of the programme, and one which students find both enjoyable and informative.

composed

The full time course is made up of six modules, each of wh may be studied seperately on a p/t basis. Completion of all 6 modules, lead to the award of the Collage's Certificate in Cordon Bleu Cookery, and some of the modules will be accredited by national assessment and examining boards. *Please put words underlined in CAPS*

double line spacing

Attendance on part time programmes is from 1.00 pm to 2100 hrs one one day per week for one term. Part time students will be expected to produce written assignments and evidence of practical work done outside College, and therefore should be already employed in the Catering/Hotel industry. *Prospective students are invited to discuss this aspect with a tutor before enrolment.*

Modular Programme

Wines and Spirits

Wine tasting, labelling, viniculture.

Interior Decor

Selection and care of foliage, herbs and flowers. Colour, design, table and room settings.

Floral Art

Selection and co-ordination of fabrics and accesories *The use of* lighting and styles, *to achieve effects.*

Business Skills

The setting-up and succesfull operation of food-based entreprises

Food Hygiene

A programme leading to a nationally recognised qualification.

Task 4B cont

European Study Tour

and

An opp to compare skills/techniques, (food and wines) - and to enjoy the culture!

Save as Task 4B

<u>Prospects for Career Progression</u>

Extra paragraphs to be inserted here later - in single spacing

Task 4C

(MEMO) — use the MEMOFORM template   Please mark - BY HAND

Top + 2

To: Dave Collingridge, Services Unit
From: Veronique F___ , Accom Officer
Ref: VF/SU/9503

I understand that you have already been approached by several of our students w ref to the central heating in Ebor block. //It appears that there is a ~~timing~~ problem w the timing of the system in that the heating has been coming on ~~at~~ between 10 am and 1800 hrs whilst students are attending ~~lectures~~ courses. When the (students') return to ~~the~~ their rooms between 5 pm and 5.30 pm, the temperature is unbearably hot — ✓ ~~particularly~~ especially in good weather. However, by 10 pm the rooms are beginning to cool down and, during the ~~early hours~~ night, many students have found it too cold to sleep.   (said they)

This inefficient operation and use of resources is to the general detriment of the College, and I wd be obliged if you cd make every effort to amend the situation. It seems that two issues (needs) to be addressed — the timing and the thermostatic control of the system. //Please keep me informed of progress.

Save as Task 4C

Students have approached the Principal on this matter and so I have sent her a copy of this memo.

Task 4D

Typist/Operator: these are extra paragraphs for Task 4B

Ⓥ Former students of the College have obtained varied & interesting ~~employment~~ *work* in the running of restaurants, teaching, private catering and *freelance* chalet/yachting services. (adult classes) // 'Old' students regularly return to ~~the~~ College class rooms to pass on their experiences (usually informative, often hilarious) to our Diploma and Certificate (current) students.

Students wishing to enter higher education in the field of food technology have combined their studies w 'A' levels.

For further information, *please* ring the College Info Centre on 0904-661942

(emphasise this para)

(Save as Task 4d)

Please change 'the College' to 'the Vine Tree College' throughout

UNIT 5

Rearranging text and data

At the end of Unit 5 you will have learnt how to
- *sort items, paragraphs or lists of information into a specific order*
- *change the case of text*

Sorting (rearranging) items

There are several ways to sort or rearrange items into a particular order:

1 Before keying in the items, use a piece of scrap paper to note down, in advance, the order in which the entries should be keyed in.

2 After keying in, use normal cut-and-paste functions to sort/rearrange the items in the required order.

3 Use Word's automatic *sort* facility – see instructions under 'Sorting (rearranging) items' on next page.

Exercise 5A

5.1 Starting with a new file, key in the following exercise:

NAME	NO	D/O/B
Hardy, Anna	328	14 June 1956
Browne, Sue	147	19 May 1969
Brown, Mary	457	28 May 1957
Brown, Allen	438	15 July 1968

5.2 Using Word's automatic sort facility, practise sorting the information into

a) alphabetical order by *surname*

NAME	NO	D/O/B
Brown, Allen	438	15 July 1968
Brown, Mary	457	28 May 1957
Browne, Sue	147	19 May 1969
Hardy, Anna	328	14 June 1956

b) ascending numerical order by *number*

NAME	NO	D/O/B
Browne, Sue	147	19 May 1969
Hardy, Anna	328	14 June 1956
Brown, Allen	438	15 July 1968
Brown, Mary	457	28 May 1957

c) descending date order by *D/O/B (date of birth)*

NAME	NO	D/O/B
Browne, Sue	147	19 May 1969
Brown, Allen	438	15 July 1968
Brown, Mary	457	28 May 1957
Hardy, Anna	328	14 June 1956

5.3 Start a new file – you do not need to save or print Exercise 5A.

Changing case

Word can automatically change the case of text into UPPER CASE, lower case, Sentence case, Title Case, or tOGGLE cASE. Select the text you wish to change into a different case.

Keyboard	Menu
Press: **Shift + F3** (to toggle through the different case-change options)	Select: **Format, Change Case**
	Click: On the appropriate button
Press: **Ctrl + Shift + A** (to capitalize letters)	Click: **OK**

 Sorting (rearranging) items

Word will automatically rearrange information in selected rows, lists or a series of paragraphs. The items may be sorted alphabetically, numerically or by date, and in either ascending (A-Z) or descending (Z–A) order. You can sort an entire list, or you can select just a section of it. If appropriate, you can sort a list before or after adding numbers to it – Word automatically renumbers the list if the order changes.

If two items start with the same character, Word takes account of subsequent characters in each item to determine the sort order. If an entire field is the same for two items, Word takes account of subsequent fields specified to determine the sort order, e.g. surnames and first names.

- Select: The items or text to be sorted
- Select: **Table, Sort Text** (if the items are in a table the command name changes to **Sort**)

The **Sort** dialogue box is displayed on screen:

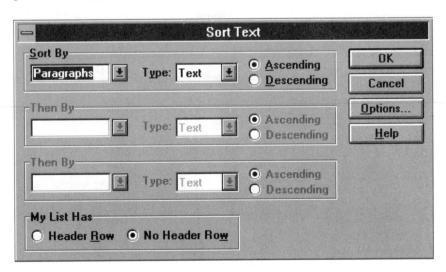

Select from the sort dialogue options as appropriate:

Sort by	Select paragraphs or a field number - you can sort up to three fields or criteria
Then By	You may specify subsequent sort criteria for additional fields/columns by entering further sort criteria in the **Then By** boxes
Type	Select type of information to be sorted – text, numbers or dates. Word will accept several different date formats, e.g. Jan 27 1995, 27 Jan 1995, Jan-95, 1-27-95, 1/27/95, 1-27-95
Header Row	If the selection includes a heading(s) which you don't want to be sorted choose this option button – Word will exclude the heading(s) from the sort (alternatively, miss out any headings when you select the items to be sorted)

Ascending   To sort in ascending order, e.g. A–Z, 1-100, 1 January 19xx – 31 December 19xx

Descending   To sort in descending order, e.g. Z–A,100-1, 31 December 19xx – 1 January 19xx

<u>**O**</u>**ptions**   To change the field delimeter – type or select the appropriate separator character, then choose the **OK** button

OK   Click: **OK** to operate the sort

Undo sort   Click: The **Undo** button on the Standard Tool Bar

---

Exercise 5B

5.4   Starting a new file, key in the following exercise. Amend as shown. Save and print your document using filename **EX5B**. Check your print-out with that at the back of the book and correct any errors.

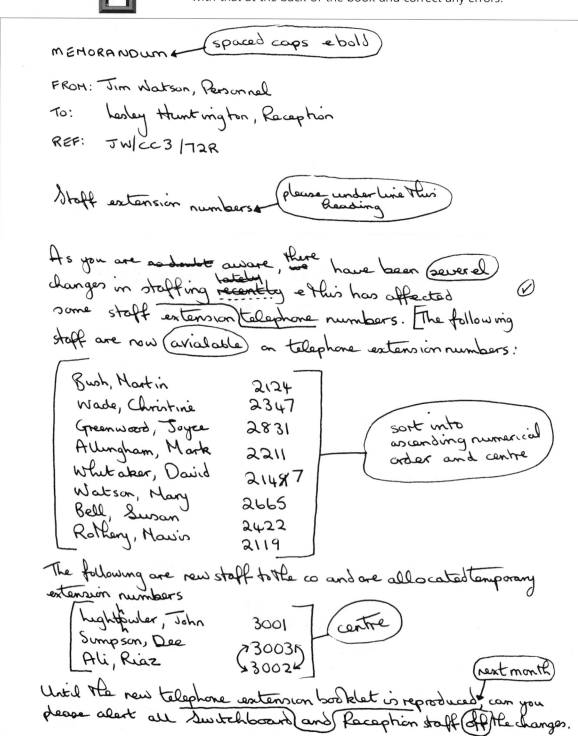

Exercise 5C

5.5 Retrieve the file **EX5B** if it is not already on screen:

- Sort the list of telephone extension numbers into alphabetical order of **surname**
- Save and print your document using filename **EX5C**
- Check your print-out with that at the back of the book and correct any errors

Exercise 5D

5.6 Retrieve the file **EX5C** if it is not already on screen:

- Amend as indicated
- Sort the list of telephone extension numbers into alphabetical order of **department**
- Save and print your document using filename **EX5D**
- Check your print-out with that at the back of the book and correct any errors

---

M E M O R A N D U M ← *(centre)*

FROM: Jim Watson, Personnel

TO: Lesley Huntington, Reception

REF: JW/CC3/72R

DATE: today's

(change to uppercase)

Staff extension numbers

As you are aware, there have been several changes in staffing recently and this has affected some staff telephone extension numbers.

The following staff are now available on telephone extension numbers:

DEPARTMENT	NAME	EXT NO
Stores	Allingham, Mark	2211
Sales	Bell, Susan	2422
Reception	Bush, Martin	2124
Text Production	Greenwood, Joyce	2831
Personnel	Rothery, Mavis	2119
Catering	Wade, Christine	2347
Sales	Watson, Mary	2665
Administration	Whitaker, David	2147

operator:
a) move this section back to left margin
b) delete any line spaces between the two lists so they become one
c) sort into alphabetical order by DEPARTMENT

~~The following are new staff to the company and are allocated temporary extension numbers:~~

Marketing	Ali, Riaz	3003
Computing	Lighthowler, John	3001
Purchasing	Simpson, Dee	3002

Until the new telephone extension booklet is reproduced next month, can you please alert all Reception and Switchboard staff of the changes. ← *change this sentence to uppercase and centre*

leave ½" (12mm) clear vertical space here

5.7 Exit the program if you have finished working or continue straight on to the next unit.

UNIT 6 *Tables*

At the end of Unit 6 you will have learnt how to
- *complete a table with subdivided columns and multi-line headings*
- *rearrange/sort items in the table into a specified order*
- *use Word's automatic Table Wizard facility to produce table layouts*

Tabulation

Data is often presented in columns within letters, memos and reports to convey information quickly and clearly. Tabulated columns of information are also used for separate tables and accounts. (If you align text on screen by pressing the spacebar, rather than using tab stops, it may not line up when you print.) On some keyboards the tab key is labelled **Tab** and on others shown as ⇄

In Word for Windows the tab settings are normally defaulted (i.e. previously set) to every 0.5 inch. Each time you press the tab key you indent the line by 0.5 inch. You can often complete a table satisfactorily using the default tabs. There will be times, however, especially if you are typing a table with columns containing a lot of data, where space is limited, or when you need to include subdivided or multi-line column headings, when you will need to *set, delete* or *change* the position of the default tab settings.

As an alternative to normal tabulation procedures, Word for Windows has an automatic Table Wizard facility which you can use to produce table layouts (see instructions following).

If the table is quite large, you may also need to give consideration to making it fit on the page/paper size being used. If you think the table won't fit using normal settings, you could:

- reduce the left and right margins to ¹/₂ inch – this is the least amount acceptable
- wrap the text around on to the next line in the column
- reduce the font size

Normal tabulation procedures - general information

- Use capitals or underlining to emphasize column headings and leave a clear line space between the heading and the information below. Leave sufficient space between the headings to allow for the longest line of each column.

- Set a tab stop for the longest line in each column, in the appropriate places, remembering to include at least three blank spaces between columns. It looks better if you leave equal amounts of space between columns but this is not absolutely necessary. (If you decide to use default tabs the spaces will probably be unequal.) Key in the columns in double or single-line spacing according to the instructions provided or amount of space available on the page.

- Depending on the type of display, you can choose a *left-aligned tab*, a *right-aligned tab*, a *decimal tab* or a *centred tab*. You can set a combination of different types of tab stops within the document and even on the same line if appropriate. For example:

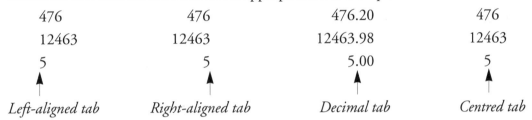

476	476	476.20	476
12463	12463	12463.98	12463
5	5	5.00	5
▲	▲	▲	▲
Left-aligned tab	*Right-aligned tab*	*Decimal tab*	*Centred tab*

- You should leave at least one clear line after the tabulation work before continuing with any further portions of text.

- If you have already keyed in your data, and you wish to add, delete or change tab stops, you should first select all the paragraphs you want to edit, then make your tab stop changes.

Creating tables: using normal tabulation procedures

- *If you have already keyed in your data:* Select all the paragraphs in which you want to add, delete or move tab stops

- *If you have **not** already keyed in your data:* Set tabs as explained below – you can always move tabs later if necessary

Mouse and ruler method

Add a tab	Click on the **Tab Alignment** button at far left of horizontal ruler until the type of tab alignment you want is displayed:
	Left-aligned tab ▣ *Decimal tab* ▣
	Right-aligned tab ▣ *Centred tab* ▣
	Click the mouse pointer on the horizontal ruler at the place where you want to set the tab stop
Delete a tab	Click and drag the tab marker off the horizontal ruler. Release the mouse button
Move a tab	Drag the tab marker to the right or left on the horizontal ruler
Change type of tab alignment	Drag the tab marker off the horizontal ruler. Follow instructions for 'add a tab'

Mouse and menu method

Select: **F̲ormat, T̲abs**. The **Tabs** dialogue box is displayed on screen,

Add a tab (complete for each tab)	Key in required position in the **T̲ab Stop Position** box (e.g. 1.5″) Select type of tab alignment from the **Alignment** box options (e.g. **L̲eft**) Click on **S̲et**. Click on **OK**
Delete a tab	Select the tab to be deleted from the **T̲ab Stop Position** box Click on **Cl̲ear**
Delete all tabs	Click on **Clear A̲ll**
Move a tab	Follow instructions for 'delete a tab' then 'add a tab' in new position
Change type of tab alignment	Highlight the tab to be changed in the **T̲ab Stop Position** box Select the new type of tab alignment from the **Alignment** box options Click on **S̲et**
Reset default tab stops	Select or key in the distance you want between tab stops in the **De̲fault Tab Stops** box (e.g. 0.5 inch). Click on **OK**

Important: Whenever you set a tab stop, you immediately cancel out any default tab stops to the *left* of it. Default tab stops to the *right* are not affected.

Creating tables: using Word's table facilities and Table Wizard

Mouse and toolbar method

- Position insertion point where you want the table to be placed
- Click: ⊞ table button on the Standard Tool Bar (a drop-down grid of rows and column cells appears on screen)
- Select the number of rows and columns required by dragging the mouse pointer across the grid until the bottom of the grid displays the correct layout (e.g. 3 x 4 table). The grid will increase in size as you drag the mouse. Release the mouse button

1 Table menu method   2 Table Wizard

Position insertion point where you want the table to be placed

Select: **T̲able, I̲nsert Table**

The **Insert Table** dialogue box appears on screen:

Select from the table dialogue box as appropriate:

1 **Number of <u>C</u>olumns**	Enter the required number of vertical columns
Number of <u>R</u>ows	Enter the required number of horizontal rows
Column <u>W</u>idth	Accept the default setting (**Auto**) or select a column width
	Click: **OK**

Optional:

<u>A</u>utoFormat....	The **AutoFormat** table dialogue box appears on screen Choose from the options given to specify special formatting options – the different effects available can be seen in the preview box Click: **OK** when you have made your final choices
2 **Wi<u>z</u>ard**	The Table Wizard dialogue box appears on screen. Word prompts you to choose the appropriate layout for your table: Select: <u>N</u>ext> to move to the next set of options for the table layout Select: <u>F</u>inish when your layout is complete

Note: Grey dotted guidelines will appear on screen to display the parameters of the table layout, but these will not appear on the printed copy. It is not necessary to create a table with borders for intermediate examinations – this feature will be included in the next level.

Setting tabs inside a table

You can set tabs inside a table just as you would normally. This is useful if you need to set a decimal tab or if you are working with subdivisions:

- *To set a tab for one cell only:* Set the appropriate tab-stop type on the horizontal ruler using normal tabulation procedures

- *To set a tab for a section of the table:* First select the data, then set the appropriate tab-stop type on the horizontal ruler

- *To set a tab for a whole column:* Position the insertion point in the column you want the tab stop to affect

  Select: **Select <u>C</u>olumn** from the **T<u>a</u>ble** menu, then set the appropriate tab-stop type on the horizontal ruler

Press: **Ctrl + Tab** to move to tab stops in a table (if you press the tab key on its own, you simply move to the next cell)

Remember: Whenever you set a tab stop you immediately cancel out any default tab stops set to the *left* of it. Default tabs to the *right* are unaffected.

Moving around in a table

Arrow keys	You can move around the table using the appropriate arrow keys
Tab	Moves right one cell (or inserts a new row when pressed in the last table cell)
Shift + Tab	Moves left one cell
Ctrl + Tab	Moves to next tab stop in the cell
Alt + Home	Moves to first cell in same row
Alt + End	Moves to last cell in same row
Alt + PgUp	Moves to top cell in column
Alt + PgDn	Moves to bottom cell in column

or **Click** the mouse pointer in any cell you want to move to

Changing column width in a table:

Mouse	**Menu**
• Select the column(s) to be changed	• Select the column(s) to be changed
• Point to the column dividing line and press the left mouse button down (the pointer changes to a ◄─┼─► double-headed arrow)	• Select: **Table, Cell Height and Width, Column**
• Drag the column dividing line to the left or right to increase or decrease the column width as appropriate	• Enter: The appropriate measurement in the **Width of Column** box
• Release the mouse button	• Click: **OK**
	(*Note:* You can also specify the amount of space between columns if required)

Changing row height in a table:

Mouse	**Menu**
• Select the row(s) to be changed	
• In page layout view [icon] point to row marker dividing line on vertical ruler	• Select the row(s) to be changed
	• Select: **Table, Cell Height and Width, Row**
Row marker (dividing line) *The pointer changes to a vertical double-headed arrow* ↕	• Enter: The appropriate measurement in the **Height of Rows** and **At** boxes
	• Click: **OK**
• Drag the row dividing line up or down to increase or decrease the row height as appropriate	(*Note:* You can also specify any row alignment and/or indent if required)
• Release the mouse button	

Inserting columns and rows in a table

Position the insertion point at the place you wish to make the insertion:

Select: **Table, Select Row** *or* **Select Column**

Select: **Table, Insert Rows/Insert Columns**

or Press: The right mouse button and Select: **Insert Rows/Insert Columns**

or With the insertion point in the table, click: **Table** button on Standard Tool Bar (a row is inserted above the position of the insertion point)

Deleting columns and rows in a table

Position the insertion point at the place you wish to make the deletion:

Select: **Table, Select Row** *or* **Select Column**

Select: **Table, Delete Rows/Delete Columns** *or*

Select: **Table, Delete Cells, Delete Entire Column** *or* **Delete Entire Row**

or Press: The right mouse button and select: **Delete Rows**

or Select: Column to be deleted. Press: The right mouse button and select: **Delete Columns**

Joining/merging cells in a table

Select the cells to be joined together. Select: **Table, Merge Cells**

Splitting cells in a table

Select the cells to be split. Select: **Table, Split Cells**

Subdivided and multi-line column headings

If the copy you are working from shows subdivided or multi-line column headings, remember to include these in your tab settings. Remember, even if you are using Word's table facilities you can set tabs using normal tabulation procedures within the table layout.

A *multi-line column heading* means that the column heading appears on more than one line

COURSE	START DATE	END DATE	COST £
(col.1)	(col.2)	(col.3)	(col.4)

A *subdivided column heading* means that the column heading may be divided into two or more subheadings

COURSE	COURSE DATES		COST £
	START	END	
(col.1)	(col.2 + 3)		(col.4)

If you are using Word's automatic table facility, your table layout would appear as

> *The table cells have been merged here to allow for the subdivided column heading*

COURSE	COURSE DATES		COST £
	START	END	
French	04/09/95	18/12/95	25.00
German	06/09/95	20/12/95	28.00

Practice exercise

Create a table with 4 rows and 4 columns. Practise
- moving around the table
- setting different tab types in the table
- changing the column width and row height
- inserting a row and a column
- deleting a row and a column
- entering data in the table
- joining/splitting table cells

Close the file without saving so you are ready to start the next exercise with a clear screen.

6.1 Starting with a new file, key in the following table using the font Times New Roman in font size 10. For this exercise you should use normal tabulation procedures, setting the appropriate tab stops on the horizontal ruler line – *do not use default tabs for this exercise*.

After you have keyed in the main headings, remember to enter a decimal tab so that the figures in the PRICE column will wrap around the decimal point:

Tip: Set left-aligned tab stops for CAT NO, PRICE and UNIT columns. Key in the data as shown:

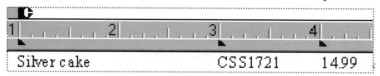

Scroll text so that line of data is just under ruler as above

Delete left-aligned tab for PRICE column

Insert decimal tab directly above decimal point in 14.99, using existing data as a guide:

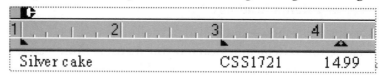

FIRTH'S FANCY GOODS

ADDITIONAL STOCK COMMODITIES

ITEM	CAT NO	PRICE £	UNIT
Cutlery			
Silver cake slicer	CSSI721	14.99	each
Silver salad servers	SSSI722	21.99	pair
Onyx-handled steak knives	SKOH723	25.99	set of 8
Silver steak knives	SKSI724	49.99	set of 8
Cruet Sets			
Silver cruet	CRSI442	14.99	set
Pottery cruet	CRPO443	5.99	set
Pine cruet	CRPI444	3.99	set
Cut-glass cruet	CRCG445	12.99	set

6.2 Save and print your document using filename **EX6A**. Check your print-out with the exercise above. If you find any errors, correct them on screen, save your document again and print again if necessary.

6.3 Retrieve EX6A if not already on your screen and carry out the following amendments:

- Move the 'Cruet' section before the 'Cutlery' section
- Change the main headings and column headings to bold text
- Rearrange the table items in alphabetical order of *item* – but keep the 'Cutlery' and 'Cruet' sections separate

*Refer back to Unit 5 for instructions on how to **sort** items.*

6.4 Save and print your document using filename **EX6B**. Check your print-out with that at the back of the book. If you find any errors, correct them on screen, save your document again and print again if necessary.

Exercise 6C

6.5 Starting with a new file, key in the following table. For this exercise, practise using Word's automatic table facility. Save and print your document using filename **EX6C**. Check your print-out with that at the back of the book. If you find any errors, correct them on screen, save your document again and print again if necessary.

Tip: Your table layout should look something like this (after sorting):

BEDLINEN ITEM	SIZE	ITEM CODE	COLOUR(S) AVAILABLE	PRICE OF ITEM USUAL £	SPECIAL £
Quilt Covers					
Zenith	SINGLE	QS241	red/white	18.99	16.99
Harlequin Court	DOUBLE	QD174	multi	29.99	24.99
Country Blossom	DOUBLE	QD183	rose	34.99	29.99

NEW BEDLINEN ITEMS ← bold

Put SIZE column items in capitals please

We have introduced recently a new selection of bedlinens into our range. In order to promote sales, they will be offered at the special/discount prices shown below: (in the table) ← indent 0.5" at left + right margins

BEDLINEN ITEM	SIZE	ITEM CODE	COLOUR(S) AVAILABLE	PRICE OF ITEM USUAL £	SPECIAL £
Quilt Covers					
Harlequin Court	Double	QD174	multi	29.99	24.99
Zenith	Single	QS241	red/white	18.99	16.99
Country Blossom	Double	QD183	rose	34.99	29.99
Valances					
Harlequin Court	Double	VD175	multi	26.99	24.99
Country Blossom	Double	VD184	rose	29.99	26.99
Zenith	Single	VS242	red/white	16.99	14.99
Pillowcases					
Z____	n/a	P243	s/white	5.99	5.50
C___ B___	n/a	P185	rose	7.99	6.99
H____ C___	n/a	P176	multi	6.99	5.99

please sort by order of item "special" price within each section — ensure all corresponding data columns are re arranged

The "special" prices will be offered until the end of next month and then the usual price will apply.

Exercise 6D

6.6 Starting with a new file, key in the following table. You may design the table layout either by using normal tabulation procedures or by using Word's automatic table facility. Save and print your document using filename **EX6D**. Check your print-out with that at the back of the book. If you find any errors, correct them on screen, save your document again and print again if necessary.

WORK EXPERIENCE ← (centre + bold)

(please sort into alphabetical order of surname within each section — ensure all the corresponding details are rearranged)

TRAINEE DETAILS

If any trainees are unable to complete their work experience on the dates shown they should notify their Course Tutor immed.

(change surnames only to CAPITAL letters)

NAME OF TRAINEE	ENROLMENT CODE	NAME OF ORGANISATION	WORK EXPERIENCE DATES	
			START	FINISH
Business Studies				
Milnes, Mary	34278 6	B R Stubbs Ltd	14 Oct	18 Oct
Bray, Anthony	36121	Haye + Lund Ltd	14 Oct	18 Oct
Ashton, Joe	37229	Haye + Lund Ltd	7 Oct	18 Oct
Singh, Jared	36145	J Spencer + Son	14 Oct	18 Oct
Dawley, Lisa	35127	William Dykes	21 Oct	28 Oct
Jarvis, Rita	33345	B Simms	7 Oct	18 Oct
Catering				
Haugh, Paula	36672	Astoria Hotel	31 Oct	4 Nov
Watts, ~~Emma~~ Evie	36761	Richmond Hotel	7 Nov	11 Nov
Brown, Sheila	35227	Verdi's Restaurant	7 Nov	18 Nov
Townsend, Paul	35219	Susi's Bistro	31 Nov	4 Nov
Art and Design				
Amy, Hughes	36299	V J Designs Ltd	14 Oct	18 Oct
Rent, Sally	34117	Century Graphics	7 Oct	18 Oct
Iqbal, Abdul	36221	Says Art Decor	31 Oct	4 Nov

(please move Art and Design to become the first section)

(embolden all the words marked with a X)

(retain the abbreviations for the months)

(TIP: it is unlikely that the table will work using default tabs and you may need to change the margins)

UNIT 7 *Standard paragraphs*

At the end of Unit 7 you will have learnt how to
- *store standard paragraphs or portions of text for repeated use*
- *insert standard paragraphs or portions of text into a document as required*
- *use the AutoText feature on Word for Windows*
- *compose a standard letter*

You will need to refresh your memory on
- *business letter layout and routeing copies*
- *changing your right margin or indenting text from the right*

i Boilerplating and standard letters

Many letters or documents have some parts in them that are identical in content. This can mean keying in the same portions of text over and over again, e.g. company addresses, standard paragraphs or the salutation at the end. In Word for Windows you can store text or graphics that you use repeatedly and insert them as required into any document. This can obviously save you a great deal of keying-in time. It is often called 'boilerplating'.

There are several methods of boilerplating in Word. You can use the AutoText feature button on the Standard Tool Bar to store and insert standard portions of text and/or graphics – see method B. AutoText allows you to save all your standard paragraphs in one master file. Or you can save the standard paragraphs as individuals files, using normal save procedures, and insert them into your main document as required – see method A. If you are inserting items which have been saved previously by someone else, you will need to identify the method by which they have been stored.

Standard letters need to be well displayed. You should standardize on layout, line spacing and heading styles. You may need to emphasize text (bold, underline, etc.), extract information from another task and route copies. Also, don't forget to insert the date in the correct position.

Boilerplating using standard files: method A

Store standard paragraphs as individual files:

* Key in the portion of text to be saved as a standard paragraph file.

* Save as a separate file in the usual way by selecting **Save As** from the **File** menu, then enter an appropriate filename. (If you use easily identifiable filenames it will help you to retrieve the correct file, e.g. **SINCE** for a Yours sincerely closure, or **FAITH** for a Yours faithfully closure).

Insert the standard paragraph file into your document:

* Position the cursor at the place where you want the standard paragraph file to be inserted.

* Retrieve the standard paragraph file by selecting **File** from the **Insert** menu, then select or key in the appropriate filename you wish to insert. Click on **OK**.

Boilerplating using AutoText : method B

Create an AutoText entry:

* Key in the text you wish to store as a standard paragraph/item, then select (highlight) it

* Click: the AutoText button on the Standard Tool Bar

  or Select: **AutoText** from the **Edit** menu

The **AutoText** dialogue box appears on screen:

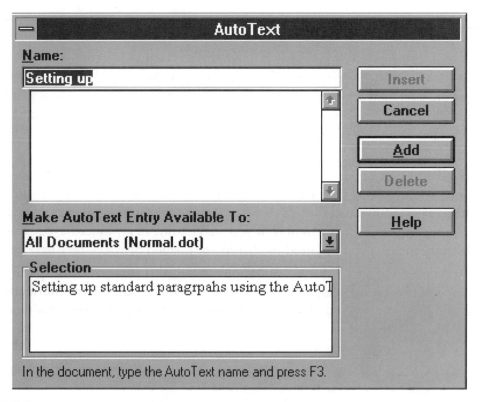

* Word suggests a name for the selection in the **Name** box – you can overtype with a name of your own choice if you wish

* Click: The **Add** button to store the selected paragraph/item

(Note: You can rename, edit or delete any paragraphs/items in the AutoText dialogue box.)

Insert an AutoText entry:

* Position the cursor at the point you wish to insert the standard paragraph or item

* a) Type the *name* of the AutoText item you wish to insert

  Click: The AutoText button on the Standard Tool Bar or Press: **F3** (the item is immediately inserted into your document)

or

* b) Select: **Edit, AutoText** from the menu and select the item you wish to insert

  Click: **Formatted Text** button if you wish to retain any text formatting with the insertion, otherwise, click on the **Plain Text** button. Click: **Insert** button

---

| **Exercise 7A** | **7.1** | Starting a new file, key in the following standard paragraphs. |

* For method A, standard files, key in and save each paragraph as a separate document using the filename indicated at the left.
* For method B, AutoText, key in all the paragraphs as one document and save this under filename **AUTO1.** Then select each paragraph one at a time and store as an AutoText entry using the AutoText name indicated at the left.

Filename
or
AutoText name

Standard file or AutoText entry

ADDRESS	Firths Fancy Goods
	147 Stanningley Road
	LEEDS
	LO3 4TR
	Tel No: 0532 672471
ORDER	We were pleased to receive your recent order for a selection of our fancy goods.
ENQUIRY	Thank you for your recent enquiry regarding our range of fancy goods.
INSTOCK	The goods you have requested are in stock and will be despatched within the next fourteen days.
OUTSTOCK	We regret to advise you that the goods are currently out of stock.
PRICE	Please find enclosed our new price list and latest catalogue.
SINCE	Yours sincerely FIRTHS FANCY GOODS Sales Department
FAITH	Yours faithfully FIRTHS FANCY GOODS Sales Department

Exercise 7B

7.2 Starting a new file, key in the letter below with a ragged right margin. As you key in the letter, retrieve the relevant standard paragraphs using the filenames or AutoText names shown (e.g. **ADDRESS**) at the appropriate marked points.

Save and print your document using filename **EX7B**. Check your printout with that at the back of the book. If you find any errors, retrieve the document and correct.

(ADDRESS)

today's date

Mr B Waverley
Glen Cottage
Glen Crescent
BURNLEY
BR5 2LN

Dear Mr Waverley

please emphasize this heading

Re: your order of 22 November 1994
(ORDER)
The goods you have requested are:

a)   I earthen ware breadcrock @ £7.99 each.

b)   2 silver cruet sets @ £ *(refer to Exercise 6A for this information)* set ~~each~~.

(INSTOCK)

access   *a rec for wh*

Thank you for your payment by ~~cheque~~ is enclosed with this letter.

(PRICE) We look forward to offering our services to you again in the near future.

(SINCE)

Encs

Exercise 7C

7.3 Starting a new file, key in the letter below with a justified right margin. Retrieve the relevant standard paragraphs using the filenames or AutoText names shown at the appropriate marked points.

Save and print your document using filename **EX7C**. Check your print-out with that at the back of the book. If you find any errors, retrieve the document and correct.

(ADDRESS)

Mrs L Anwar
37 Burberry Place
BURBERRY
BB5 4TL

Dear Mrs A _____

OPERATOR:

• emphasize the words underlined with ~~~

• all paragraphs to be in same style as the paragraph beginning "Please accept our..."

(ORDER)

Your order included:

a)   1 set of *(refer to Ex 6A for this information)* -handled steak knives @ £25.99 per set of 8.

b)   3 satin-edged hand towels in blue @ £4.99 each.

(OUTSTOCK)

It seems that your order was taken ~~fom~~ from an out of date cat. (PRICE)

leave a space here 2" across by 1" down (51mm × 25mm) for a voucher

We will be pleased to supply you with alternative items from the new cat or offer ~~offer~~ you a full refund.

for any incon caused

Please accept our apologies, along with the attached £2 voucher wh you may use towards the cost of your replacement goods.

(SINCE)

Encs

Exercise 7D

7.4 Starting a new file, key in the letter below with a ragged right margin. Retrieve the relevant standard paragraphs using the filenames or AutoText names shown at the appropriate marked points.

Save and print your document using filename **EX7D**. Check your print-out with that at the back of the book. If you find any errors, retrieve the document and correct.

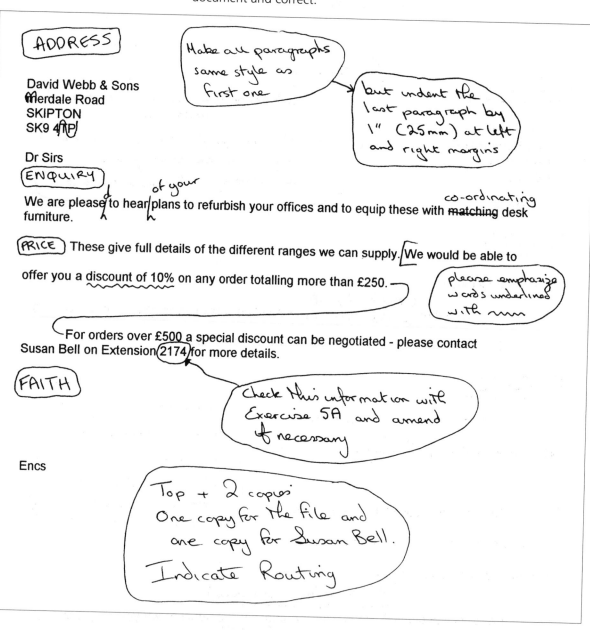

7.5 Exit the program if you have finished working or continue straight on to the next unit.

Consolidation 2

Key in the following standard paragraphs. Save each one under filename or AutoText name shown.

Filename or AutoText name	Standard file or AutoText entry
TRAINING	Thank you for your recent application for staff training.
FORM	In order to process your application, could you please complete the green Form STA/4, for which you will also need the signature of your line manager.
OPEN LEARNING	We have a number of open learning packages which you can work through at your own pace using a PC.

Key in the document below with a ragged right margin. Insert the relevant phrases at the points marked. Save and print your document using filename **TASK8B**. Check your print-out with that at the back of the book. If you find any errors, correct them on screen, save your document again and print again if necessary.

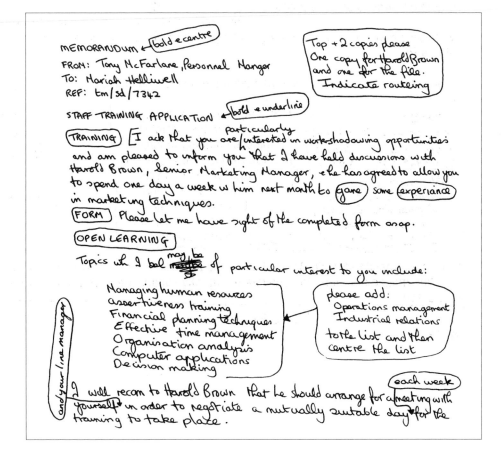

Task 8C

Retrieve the file TASK8B if it is not already on your screen. Amend the document as indicated in the draft below and also:

- change the right margin to justified
- adjust the typing line length for the whole document to 5 inches
- replace **Harold Brown** with **Harry Browne** throughout the document
- insert **STAFF TRAINING** to appear as a header at top right on every page
- put page numbering at bottom right of the page – do not number the first page

---

MEMORANDUM

add this section to ✱✱

FROM: Tony McFarlane, Personnel Manager

TO: Mariah Helliwell

REF: tm/sd/7342 → *copy to end of document*

DATE: today's

STAFF TRAINING APPLICATION ← *centre*

If next month is uncon for yr training to take place, I wd suggest that you take the following action:
a) notify yr line manager immed
b) indicate on Form STA/4 an alternative date, or
c) call to see me personally to discuss your requirements

Thank you for your recent application for staff training.

I acknowledge that you are particularly interested in work-shadowing opportunities and am pleased to inform you that I have held discussions with Harold Brown, Senior Marketing Manager, and he has agreed to allow you to spend one day a week with him next month to gain some experience in marketing techniques.

✱
In order to process your application, could you please complete the green Form STA/4, for which you will also need the signature of your line manager. Please let me have sight of the completed form as soon as possible. *leave at least 1" (25mm) clear space here* ↑

We have a number of open learning packages which you can work through at your own pace using a PC.

Topics which I believe may be of particular interest to you include:

Operator:
a) remove centring and indent the left-aligned list 1½" (37mm) from left margin
b) sort the list into alphabetical order
c) change to double line spacing

→ Managing human resources
Assertiveness training
Financial planning techniques
Effective time management
Organisation analysis
Computer applications
Decision making
Operations management
Industrial relations

Save + Print the file using filename: TASK 8C (you only need to print one top copy)

I will recommend to Harold Brown that he should arrange for a meeting with yourself and your line manager in order to negotiate a mutually suitable day each week for the training to take place.

move to ✱

✱ ✱

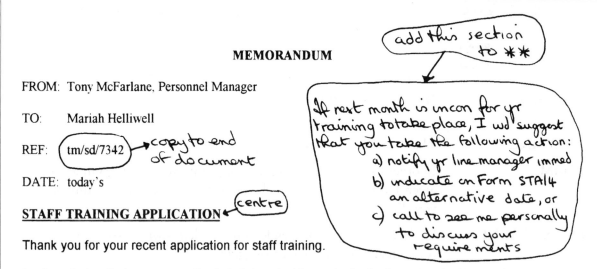

Task 8D

Key in the following table. Save and print your document using filename **TASK8D**. Check your print-out with that at the back of the book. If you find any errors, correct them on screen, save your document again and print again if necessary.

Staff Training Sessions
Draft for March

(caps, centre and bold)

(please move this paragraph to ✱ and indent by ½" (12mm) at left and right margins)

NB: Please note that Training Session A34, Switchboard Training, is for the ~~newly~~ ~~not~~ ~~added~~ switchboard system to be installed in April — training is, therefore, restricted to the Reception Team only.

TRAINING SESSION	VENUE/ ROOM	DATE	CODE	TRAINING SESSION TIMES	
				START	FINISH
I.T. APPLICATIONS					
Networking	A29	15 March	IT47	9.00am	5.00pm
Advanced ~~DTP~~ DTP	A29	29 M —	IT48	9.00am	5.00 pm
Database	A29	22 M —	IT49	9.00am	12.30pm
Introduction to CD-Rom	A42	8 M —	IT50	1.30 pm	5.00 pm
ADMINISTRATIVE					
Audio Training Day	Main Office	28M—	A32	9.00am	5.00 pm
Management Up-date	Conference	21 M —	A34	1.30 pm	5.00pm
Switchboard Training	Reception	9 M —	A33	9.00 am	12.30 pm
MISCELLANEOUS					
Health and Safety	Boardroom	10M—	M62	9.00am	12.30pm
Assertiveness Training	Boardroom	3 M —	M63	9.00am	12.30pm
Time Organisation	Conference	30M—	M65	1.30 pm	5.00 pm
Public Speaking	Conference	17M —	M64	1.30 pm	5.00 pm

✱ *(please place the CODE column before the VENUE/ROOM column)*

operator:
- *put all words underlined with ﹌ in bold text*
- *rearrange in ascending date order of DATE for each section. Ensure all corresponding details are also rearranged*

UNIT 9 *Examination practice*

Key in the following standard paragraphs. Save each one under filename or AutoText name shown.

Filename or AutoText name	*Standard file or AutoText entry*
CUSTOMER	Our basic philosophy is to take every possible step to match all aspects of our business with customer satisfaction.
VALUE	Our entire range of products provides the best value for money and performance available.
SERVICE	As we are a British company with over 20 years' experience in the computing industry, you can trust in our proven record of providing reliable and quality services.
WARRANTY	All our systems carry a 12-month warranty for parts and labour including collection from, and return to, your own home.

Task 9B

Key in the letter below with a ragged right margin. Save and print your document using filename **TASK9B** – print the letter on the letterhead for Tower Computers included in this book. Check your print-out with that at the back of the book. If you find any errors, correct them on screen, save your document again and print again if necessary.

Our ref   GJ/72F

Miss Jane Hunter
42 Appleby Rd
BATH
BA8 4GT

mark this URGENT

Dr Miss H——

I have recieved yr recent enquiry about purchasing a computer from our co.// I am delighted to hear that you consider us to be a leading mfr in the computing field. I will tried to let you have as much info as poss. We like to give our cleints every opp to select the most appropriate equipment for there needs and at the expence they can best afford.

One of our Sales Representatives, Simon De Vere, will be in yr area soon e wd be able to make an appt to see you on (give date for first Monday of next month). Simon wd be able to demonstrate several (model) in yr own home. [In the meantime, please find (enclose) this (years') new (catalog) w details of our full range of systems along with a number of misc products.

Yrs scly

Gareth Jones (Sales Administrator)

Task 9C

Retrieve the file TASK9B if it is not already on your screen. Insert the relevant phrases at the points marked as shown below. Save and print your document using filename **TASK9C** – print the letter on the Tower Computers letterhead included in this book. Check your print-out with that at the back of the book. If you find any errors, correct them on screen, save your document again and print again if necessary.

Our ref GJ/72f

today's date

URGENT

Miss Jane Hunter
42 Appleby Road
BATH
BA8 4GT

Dear Miss Hunter

I have received your recent enquiry about purchasing a computer from our company.

Insert phrase stored as CUSTOMER

I am delighted to hear that you consider us to be a leading manufacturer in the computing field. I will try to let you have as much information as possible. We like to give our clients every opportunity to select the most appropriate equipment for their needs and at the expense they can best afford *Insert phrase stored as VALUE*

Insert phrase stored as WARRANTY

One of our Sales Representatives, Simon De Vere, will be in your area soon and would be able to make an appointment to see you on *(date for first Monday of next month)*. Simon would be able to demonstrate several models in your own home.

Insert phrase stored as SERVICE

In the meantime, please find enclosed this year's new catalogue with details of our full range of systems along with a number of miscellaneous products.

Yours sincerely

Gareth Jones
Sales Administrator

Enc

Task 9D

Key in the document below. Save and print your document using filename **TASK9D**. Check your print-out with that at the back of the book. If you find any errors, correct them on screen, save your document again and print again if necessary.

MEMORANDUM ← (bold + centre)

From: Gareth Jones, Sales Administrator
To: Zandra Holstedt, Rep Supervisor
Ref: GJ/SR/47

SALES REP VISITS

operator: in the DATE column,
- Please replace * with the name of next month (eg May) and replace ** with this year (eg 1995)
- retain the date format shown (eg dd/mm/yy)

Following a (numbers) of customer enquiries/recd recently, I have arranged for sales reps appts to take place on the dates shown in the table below (if) any dates are (inconveneint) please let me know asap thro' normal channels so that I may have suff time to arrange an ~~other alternative~~ date with the customer.

CUSTOMER NAME	CUSTOMER ADDRESS DETAILS STREET/ROAD etc	TOWN	TELEPHONE NO	DATE
Rep: Simon DeVere				
Leigh, Vera	26 Scarbottom Rd	BURY	0798 364792	26/*/**
Middleton, Sam	49 Highway Cresc	LEEDS	0532 579241	7/*/**
Hunter, Jane	← see TASK9B →		0225 577711	see Task 9B
Nazir, Ashraf	14 Regents Clo	BURY	0798 465232	9/*/**
Rep: Mila Yokovic				
Wood, Jordan	9 Waverley Pl	YORK	0904 562212⁴	27/*/**
Roberts, Jan	17 Exmoor St	YORK	0904 497733	8/*/**
Grimes, Henry	77 Lister Rd	YORK	0904 621721	17/*/**
Rep: Lydia Austin				
Fenney, Ian	58 Astral Ave	MIRFIELD	0924 677541	12/*/**
Shafiq, Mohammed	62 Turner View	GRIMSBY	0472 566222	13/*/**
Dobson, Marie	2 Kirkdale Rd	MIRFIELD	0924 347718	22/*/**
James, William	20 Bethel St	GRIMSBY	0472 358211	19/*/**

please embolden the Rep: names for each section

NB: you may retain the abbreviation Rep throughout

arrange in alphabetical order of surname for each Rep. Ensure all the corresponding details are also rearranged accordingly

Task 9E

Key in the document below. Save and print your document using filename **TASK9E**. Check your print-out with that at the back of the book. If you find any errors, correct them on screen, save your document again and print again if necessary.

SOME 'INSIDE' ~~INFORMATION~~ **INFORMATION**

COMPUTER HARDWARE

(double-line spacing please)

(make all subheadings the same style as the last one: HARD DISK)

There are now numerous clones of the IBM PC on the market and/with such a wide choice, [its] often difficult for the average consumer to know what/to look for. *faced* *specifications*

Purchasing the ~~wrong~~ *right* hardware and software could be a costly business so it's worth [spend;ing] some time checking out the basic details. ✓

Processor

The processor is imp[ro]tant because it determines the speed at which your system will operate. [Fro] modern software you will need at least a 386 processor, ~~with prices falling,~~ although a 486 or better would be [preferable.Remember] also that a DX machine is faster than an SX.

Another factor [afecting] speed is the 'clock speed' usually quoted in megahertz (MHz). This indicates the number of software instructions that the pro cessor can handle per second. The more the MHz the faster the processor will run.

Processor Upgradeable

With technology so rapidly moving, it can be worth considering a 'processor-upgradeable' PC - the processor is/mounted in a removable card which can be traded in later for something more [powerfull] A disadvantage is that they can be/expensive . *very*

(START A NEW PAGE HERE)

HARD DISK

A hard disk [are] usually "fixed" inside /the PC and [provide] [permenant] storage for programs and data.

❋ *(soon)*
That may seem a lot, but when you realise that a single advanced application can/easily eat up 5Mb-10Mb <u>before</u> you even begin to work on it, it's easy to see how you could fill a 40 Mb hard disk. Get the best hard disk you can afford. *Altho' it's possible to upgrade, it's both costly & disruptive.*

(The storage capacity of a hard disk is measured in megabytes (Mb).)

(One megabyte can store approx a million characters of text, numbers or program code etc.)

(insert this paragraph at ❋)

~~operator:~~ Key in in double line spacing
• make all the subheadings the same style as Processor Upgradeable

Task 9F

Retrieve the file TASK9E if it is not already on your screen and follow the amendments shown in the copy below. Change the right margin to justified. Adjust the typing line length to 5 inches (12.5 cm). Save and print your document using filename **TASK9F**. Check your print-out with that at the back of the book. If you find any errors, correct them on screen, save your document again and print again if necessary.

COMPUTER HARDWARE

SOME 'INSIDE' INFORMATION

bold & centre

insert BASIC SYSTEM INFORMATION to appear as a header on every page

There are now numerous clones of the IBM PC on the market and faced with such a wide choice, it's often difficult for the average consumer to know what specifications to look for.

Purchasing the wrong hardware and software could be a costly business so it's worth spending some time checking out the basic details.

this section in single line spacing

leave at least 3" (76mm) clear vertical space here

(A)
PROCESSOR

should be a prime factor

The processor ~~is important~~ because it determines the speed at which your system will operate. For modern software you will need at least a 386 processor, although a 486 or better would be preferable. Remember also that a DX machine is faster than an SX.

Another factor affecting speed is the 'clock speed' usually quoted in megahertz (MHz). This indicates the number of software instructions that the processor can handle per second. The more the MHz the faster the processor will run.

Copy the first paragraph beginning "Purchasing the wrong ------" to (B) and indent ½" (12 mm) at left and right margins. Retain single line spacing

PROCESSOR UPGRADEABLE

may

With technology moving so rapidly, it ~~can~~ be worth considering a 'processor-upgradeable' PC ~~the processor is mounted in a removable card which can be traded in later for something more powerful~~. A disadvantage is that they can be very expensive.

move this section to (A)

HARD DISK

A hard disk is usually 'fixed' inside the PC and provides permanent storage for programs and data. The storage capacity of a hard disk is measured in megabytes (Mb).

One megabyte can store approximately a million characters of text, numbers or program code etc.

That may seem ~~a lot~~ *excessive*, but when you realise that a single advanced ~~application~~ *software program* can easily eat up 5Mb-10Mb <u>before</u> you even begin to work on it, it's easy to see how you could soon fill a 40Mb hard disk. ~~Get~~ *In the long run it makes good sense to buy* the best hard disk you can afford. ~~Although it's possible to upgrade, it's both costly and disruptive.~~

Memory

Random access memory (RAM) is necy to store programs + data whilst they are in use. Memory is also measured in Mb and if you are using Microsoft Windows you need a lot of it! Ideally, a well-designed PC should have room to expand to 32Mb or even 64Mb with at least 8Mb on the main board.

SCREENS

Nowadays, VGA (video graphics adapter) is the minimum screen display to select with its image of 640 by 48 points (pixels) in 16 colours or 320 x 200 points in 256 colours. Altho' VGA is good enough for most users, you can get SVGA (Super VGA) with even higher resolutions of around 1024 by 768 and more colours. [If you are buying on a shoestring, you can save money with a monochrome screen - most applications don't need to be run in colour.

(B)   *change PC to Personal Computer throughout this document*

start the section headed SCREENS on a new page

VINE TREE COLLEGE

GRAPES LANE
GLASSINGTON
YORK YO6 9RW

❖❖❖❖❖❖❖❖❖❖❖❖❖❖❖   TEL: 0904-661942 FAX: 0904-345434   ❖❖❖❖❖❖❖❖❖❖❖❖❖❖❖

Tower Computers

19 Greendale Road
HALIFAX
Tel No: 0422 378541

UNIT TWO

Printing/Text Production
Unit 2   Wordway Park   DURHAM   DM10 8JJ
Tel: 091-887766   Fax: 091-765439

Print-out checks

Exercise 1A

PRODUCING PERFECT COPY

It is easy to think that, because you have used the spelling tool in Word for Windows, your work is accurate. Automatic spelling checks are very useful and you should always use them if they are available on your system, before you save or print a document but you must *also* proofread the document yourself.

Candidates who fail examinations often do so because their proofreading is not adequate. One of the most common errors is the omission of words. Unfortunately, if you have missed out some words, or not deleted some words as instructed, spellchecking will not detect this.

If you have typed the wrong 'version' of a word, eg **there** instead of **their**, spelling check will not detect this as both versions are spelt correctly. However, Word's grammar tool should detect the error and suggest the correct version to you.

Only *you* can tell if you have copied names of people or places correctly and if a piece of information which you were asked to find is accurate. For example, spellcheck cannot tell if the date you have keyed in for 'Thursday of next week' is the correct one. Don't guess - use a diary or calendar. To check up on today's date, you could use Word's Date and Time facility which is found under the Insert Menu. (The current time is displayed on the Status Bar at the bottom of the screen.)

The skills of proofreading are essential in text processing. You should train yourself to check every detail in any work you have done before you print it so as not to waste paper. It is not enough to check the work on your screen, you must compare it with the 'copy' from which you are working - going through it word by word.

Exercise 1C

Top Jobs Employment Agency

A new employment agency has placed an advertisement in the local evening newspaper. Both temporary and permanent positions are processed by the agency and they announce that they have sufficient contacts and experience to accommodate requests from a wide range of businesses and clients. A colleague of mine recommended the agency. She achieved her aim of getting a responsible job dealing with committee work and corresponding with foreign companies in the financial field.

If you are looking for a new post, you could save some expense and inconvenience through the use of an agency.

Although a fee is charged for the service, you will receive access to a range of jobs and there will be an opportunity to discuss your previous learning and achievements with experienced staff who appreciate your skills and who will take definite steps to develop your curriculum vitae and help you to prepare for an interview. The agency staff may be able to recommend a career move or a course of learning which may not have been obvious to you.

Most agencies at present have plenty of openings for:

Personal Assistants/Senior Secretaries

Administrators at all levels
WP Operators
Book-keeping/accounts clerks.

Exercise 1D

Creating a good impression

When you apply for a job, you will probably be requested to do so in the form of a letter of application (don't omit your signature) or by completing an application form, and some companies also require a curriculum vitae. After reading the advertisement, if you believe your experience is sufficient and you would like to work within the business, you should make a definite plan immediately. This is a useful exercise which forces you to assess your current position and possible action you could take to develop your career.

The presentation and content of your letter and/or curriculum vitae should be effective enough to guarantee an interview and therefore an opportunity to give a good account of yourself. Don't forget to ask permission from referees to include their name in the references section of your curriculum vitae or application form. Although most businesses acknowledge receipt of all applications in a separate letter through the post, unfortunately some do not.

If it were necessary for you to travel some distance to an interview, the organisation would normally refund your travel expenses and overnight accommodation costs.

Gather as much information as possible with reference to the business or organisation through trade catalogues and manufacturer's literature, and make sure you do not inconvenience anyone by arriving late for your appointment. Some people recommend a trial run by bus or train in order to estimate the approximate travelling time and become familiar with the route.

Exercise 1E

Top Jobs Employment Agency

A new employment agency has placed an advertisement in the local evening newspaper. Both temporary and permanent positions are processed by the agency and they announce that they have sufficient contacts and experience to accommodate requests from a wide range of businesses and clients. A colleague of mine recommended the agency. She achieved her aim of getting a responsible job dealing with committee work and corresponding with foreign companies in the financial field.

If you are looking for a new post, you could save some expense and inconvenience through the use of an agency.

Although a fee is charged for the service, you will receive access to a range of jobs and there will be an opportunity to discuss your previous learning and achievements with experienced staff who appreciate your skills and who will take definite steps to develop your curriculum vitae and help you to prepare for an interview. The agency staff may be able to recommend a career move or a course of learning which may not have been obvious to you.

Most agencies at present have plenty of openings for:

Personal Assistants/Senior Secretaries
Administrators at all levels
WP Operators
Book-keeping/accounts clerks.

Exercise 1F

Creating a good impression

When you apply for a job, you will probably be requested to do so in the form of a letter of application (don't omit your signature) or by completing an application form, and some companies also require a curriculum vitae. After reading the advertisement, if you believe your experience is sufficient and you would like to work within the business, you should make a definite plan immediately. This is a useful exercise which forces you to assess your current position and possible action you could take to develop your career.

The presentation and content of your letter and/or curriculum vitae should be effective enough to guarantee an interview and therefore an opportunity to give a good account of yourself. Don't forget to ask permission from referees to include their name in the references section of your curriculum vitae or application form. Although most businesses acknowledge receipt of all applications in a separate letter through the post, unfortunately some do not.

If it were necessary for you to travel some distance to an interview, the organisation would normally refund your travel expenses and overnight accommodation costs.

Gather as much information as possible with reference to the business or organisation through trade catalogues and manufacturer's literature, and make sure you do not inconvenience anyone by arriving late for your appointment. Some people recommend a trial run by bus or train in order to estimate the approximate travelling time and become familiar with the route.

Exercise 2A

Ref ADEX/SB

(Today's date)

URGENT

Mr Martin Wise
Top Jobs Employment Agency
Occupation House
South Place
DARLINGTON
DN3 5ON

Dear Mr Wise

ADVERTISING LITERATURE

Further to our recent conversation at the ADEX Show, I have pleasure in enclosing our catalogue which gives full information on our wide range of services.

Our organisation has invested in the latest technology in order to realise the highest quality work and this investment has paid off - a 25% increase in business over the past 6 months and a predicted rise of over 30% in the coming 12 months.

The 'Hi-flyers' range which I mentioned as a possible solution to your company are available in two sizes - A4 (210mm by 297mm) and A5 (149mm by 210mm). Paper used may be 80gsm or 100gsm.

Costs range from £25.50 to £50.00 per thousand, depending on the quality, complexity and size of the art work. If colour printing is requested, the price would start at around £35.00. This is merely an approximate guide and we can discuss financial details when we meet.

I realise that it is necessary for us to get together as soon as possible so I have asked my secretary - Maria Calder - to ring you to arrange a definite appointment for me to visit your office with our presentation portfolio. I could be with you between 9.30 am and 4.30 pm from Monday to Wednesday: from Thursday to Saturday I am based at the Sunderland office. I hope to see you in the near future.

Yours sincerely

Susanne Beaumont

Enc

Exercise 2C

MEMORANDUM

TO: Flora Sim, Training Officer

FROM: Edward Dent, Health and Safety Officer

REF: ED/HS/Training

DATE: *(date of typing)*

CONFIDENTIAL

HEALTH AND SAFETY TRAINING

Recent European directives have highlighted areas of concern for small and medium-sized companies, and I was asked to organise a thorough survey of the whole organisation to identify any problem areas.

Although employees must be consulted and their proposals should be considered, it is the employer's absolute responsibility to avoid, evaluate and combat all risks. Work conditions and systems must be adapted to suit individual and group needs. Occupations involving specific hazards must have those hazards clearly identified and explained to employees, and employers are obliged to ensure that any recommended measures are implemented immediately.

The main risks have been identified and evaluated and, in the majority of cases, only minor improvements are necessary. If you are interested, I would be pleased to explain my findings and discuss these with you.

The Health and Safety Action Plan is to be circulated within the next few days. Training will, of course, form a large part of the plan and I would like to organise the implementation of this with you.

I will be on holiday until Monday *(1st Monday of next month)*. Please telephone me on my return.

Exercise 2D

UNIT TWO

Printing/Text Production

Unit 2 Wordway Park DURHAM DM10 8JJ

Tel: 091-887766   Fax: 091-765439

Ref ADEX/SB

(Today's date)

URGENT

Mr Martin Wise
Top Jobs Employment Agency
Occupation House
South Place
DARLINGTON
DN3 5ON

Dear Mr Wise

ADVERTISING LITERATURE

Further to our recent conversation at the ADEX Show, I have pleasure in enclosing our catalogue which gives full information on our wide range of services.

Our organisation has invested in the latest technology in order to realise the highest quality work and this investment has paid off - a 25% increase in business over the past 6 months and a predicted rise of over 30% in the coming 12 months.

The 'Hi-flyers' range which I mentioned as a possible solution to your company are available in two sizes - A4 (210mm by 297mm) and A5 (149mm by 210mm). Paper used may be 80gsm or 100gsm.

Costs range from £25.50 to £50.00 per thousand, depending on the quality, complexity and size of the art work. If colour printing is requested, the price would start at around £35.00. This is merely an approximate guide and we can discuss financial details when we meet.

You expressed interest in our 'Infofolda' product which can accommodate approximately 15 to 20 pages (usually sufficient for most companies' needs). Covers are laminated and may include a stud fastening system or elasticated crossbands.

Many agencies and manufacturers recommend this folder and we believe the initial expense is justified. The materials contained in the folder can be replaced when necessary with the latest up-to-date information. The folder itself does not need to be issued every time services, prices or other details are changed. You can simply forward the separate sheets of information through the post with a covering letter.

You may recall that my colleague, Adam Randall, wished to be kept informed of our plans, so I have sent a copy of this letter to him at our Head Office. Adam has recently been appointed to Head of Marketing and he is particularly interested in our involvement in exhibitions such as the ADEX Show.

Exercise 2E

MEMORANDUM

TO: Flora Sim, Training Officer

FROM: Edward Dent, Health and Safety Officer

REF: ED/HS/Training

DATE: (date of typing)

CONFIDENTIAL

<u>HEALTH AND SAFETY TRAINING</u>

Recent European directives have highlighted areas of concern for small and medium-sized companies, and I was asked to organise a thorough survey of the whole organisation to identify any problem areas.

Although employees must be consulted and their proposals should be considered, it is the employer's absolute responsibility to avoid, evaluate and combat all risks. Work conditions and systems must be adapted to suit individual and group needs. Occupations involving specific hazards must have those hazards clearly identified and explained to employees, and employers are obliged to ensure that any recommended measures are implemented immediately.

The main risks have been identified and evaluated and, in the majority of cases, only minor improvements are necessary. If you are interested, I would be pleased to explain my findings and discuss these with you.

The Health and Safety Action Plan is to be circulated within the next few days. Training will, of course, form a large part of the plan and I would like to organise the implementation of this with you.

My preliminary ideas are given below:

Training is needed in the following areas:

1   Purchase of new machinery
2   Evaluation of existing equipment - standards and function
3   Work areas and work stations
4   Manual handling operations - 1992 regulations
5   Display screen equipment
6   Display screen operation - legal aspects
7   Personal protection - physical, chemical and biological risks
8   Equipment and machine operation
9   Signs and warnings
10 Fire extinguishers and evacuation procedures
11 First Aid
12 Hygiene
13 Handicapped workers

2

I realise that it is necessary for us to get together as soon as possible so I have asked my secretary - Maria Calder - to ring you to arrange a definite appointment for me to visit your office with our presentation portfolio. I could be with you between 9.30 am and 4.30 pm from Monday to Wednesday: from Thursday to Saturday I am based at the Sunderland office.

I hope to see you in the near future.

Yours sincerely

Susanne Beaumont

Enc

Copy: Adam Randall
        File

Routeing to Adam Randall indicated on first copy

Routeing to File indicated on second copy

Copy: Adam Randall ✓
        File

Copy: Adam Randall
        File ✓

Exercise 3A

Student Name _____ Exercise 3A _____ Centre No _____

MEMORANDUM

TO: Flora Sim, Training Officer

FROM: Edward Dent, Health and Safety Officer

REF: ED/HS/Training

DATE: *(date of typing)*

CONFIDENTIAL

HEALTH AND SAFETY TRAINING

Recent European directives have highlighted areas of concern for small and medium-sized companies, and I was asked to organise a thorough survey of the whole organisation to identify any problem areas.

Although employees must be consulted and their proposals should be considered, it is the employer's absolute responsibility to avoid, evaluate and combat all risks. Work conditions and systems must be adapted to suit individual and group needs. Occupations involving specific hazards must have those hazards clearly identified and explained to employees, and employers are obliged to ensure that any recommended measures are implemented immediately.

The main risks have been identified and evaluated and, in the majority of cases, only minor improvements are necessary. If you are interested, I would be pleased to explain my findings and discuss these with you.

The Health and Safety Action Plan is to be circulated within the next few days. Training will, of course, form a large part of the plan and I would like to organise the implementation of this with you.

My preliminary ideas are given below:

Training is needed in the following areas:

1   Purchase of new machinery
2   Evaluation of existing equipment - standards and function
3   Work areas and work stations
4   Manual handling operations - 1992 regulations
5   Display screen equipment
6   Display screen operation - legal aspects
7   Personal protection - physical, chemical and biological risks
8   Equipment and machine operation
9   Signs and warnings
10 Fire extinguishers and evacuation procedures
11 First Aid
12 Hygiene
13 Handicapped workers

I anticipate that all members of staff should receive training in items 3, 4, 7, 9, 10 and 13 above. In addition, Administrative staff should receive training in items 5 and 6. Catering staff should receive additional training in items 8 and 12. Production staff will probably need extra training in items 2 and 8. External training will be provided for first-aiders.

I would suggest that the initial phase of training should run between January - February, and should cover item 3 (Work areas and workstations), item 7 (Personal protection - physical, chemical and biological risks) and item 10 (Fire extinguishers and evacuation procedures) because the safety of personnel is paramount. The remainder of the training programme could probably be delivered between March - May. All training is to be carried out at the company's expense and during working hours.

I enclose a copy of a proposed timetable for training. Obviously, we need to discuss this in more detail. I have sent a copy of this memo to the Personnel Officer for information.

I will be on holiday until Monday *(1st Monday of next month)*. Please telephone me on my return.

Enc

Copy: Personnel Officer
          Training File

Copy: Personnel Officer ✓
          Training File

Routeing to Personnel Officer indicated on first copy

Copy: Personnel Officer
          Training File ✓

Routeing to Training File indicated on second copy

2

Exercise 3B

Ref ADEX/SB

(Today's date)

URGENT

Mr Martin Wise
Top Jobs Employment Agency
Occupation House
South Place
DARLINGTON
DN3 5ON

Dear Mr Wise

ADVERTISING LITERATURE

Further to our recent conversation at the ADEX Show, I have pleasure in enclosing our catalogue which gives full information on our wide range of services.

Our organisation has invested in the latest technology in order to realise the highest quality work and this investment has paid off - a 25% increase in business over the past 6 months and a predicted rise of over 30% in the coming 12 months.

The 'Hi-flyers' range which I mentioned as a possible solution to your company are available in two sizes - A4 (210mm by 297mm) and A5 (149mm by 210mm). Paper used may be 80gsm or 100gsm.

Costs range from £25.50 to £50.00 per thousand, depending on the quality, complexity and size of the art work. If colour printing is requested, the price would start at around £35.00. This is merely an approximate guide and we can discuss financial details when we meet.

You expressed interest in our 'Infofolda' product which can accommodate approximately 15 to 20 pages (usually sufficient for most companies' needs). Covers are laminated and may include a stud fastening system or elasticated crossbands.

Many agencies and manufacturers recommend this folder and we believe the initial expense is justified. The materials contained in the folder can be replaced when necessary with the latest up-to-date information. The folder itself does not need to be issued every time services, prices or other details are changed. You can simply forward the separate sheets of information through the post with a covering letter.

You may recall that my colleague, Adam Randall, wished to be kept informed of our plans, so I have sent a copy of this letter to him at our Head Office. Adam has recently been appointed to Head of Marketing and he is particularly interested in our involvement in exhibitions such as the ADEX Show.

Student Name   Exercise 3B   Centre No

Student Name   Exercise 3A   Centre No

I anticipate that all members of staff should receive training in items 3, 4, 7, 9, 10 and 13 above. In addition, Administrative staff should receive training in items 5 and 6. Catering staff should receive additional training in items 8 and 12. Production staff will probably need extra training in items 2 and 8. External training will be provided for first-aiders.

I would suggest that the initial phase of training should run between January - February, and should cover item 3 (Work areas and workstations), item 7 (Personal protection - physical, chemical and biological risks) and item 10 (Fire extinguishers and evacuation procedures) because the safety of personnel is paramount. The remainder of the training programme could probably be delivered between March - May. All training is to be carried out at the company's expense and during working hours.

I enclose a copy of a proposed timetable for training. Obviously, we need to discuss this in more detail. I have sent a copy of this memo to the Personnel Officer for information.

I will be on holiday until Monday *(1st Monday of next month)*. Please telephone me on my return.

Enc

Copy: Personnel Officer
         Training File

Exercise 3C

Student Name   Exercise 3C   Centre No

<u>WORKING FROM HOME</u>

Research shows that going to work causes stress and even illness. A healthy business needs healthy staff but workers are actually being made ill by factors such as traffic chaos, accidents, transport strikes and delays.

The average worker spends 2 hours a day travelling to and from their employment - an additional 25% on top of working hours. In bad weather conditions, journeys can be long and very unpleasant and the dramatically rising levels of pollution have lead to an enormous increase in the incidence of asthma. The common cold, influenza and other virus infections spread rapidly in a stuffy working environment and poor ventilation can cause sinus troubles and headaches. The country currently loses over 400 million working days through sickness per year.

A report by a management consultant for a group of bosses suggests that the solution is to allow people to work from home - 'teleworking' is the term used to describe this. It has been shown that teleworkers take less time off sick and do an average of 45% more work.

It is estimated that almost 2 million people are now working from home in Britain and they spend more than 50% of their time in doing so. They can go into the office after the rush hour and at times to suit them.

Approximately 7 in 10 bosses will try teleworking before the end of the century as developments in information technology make links between home and office more sophisticated.

TELEWORKING

I realise that it is necessary for us to get together as soon as possible so I have asked my secretary - Maria Calder - to ring you to arrange a definite appointment for me to visit your office with our presentation portfolio. I could be with you between 9.30 am and 4.30 pm from Monday to Wednesday: from Thursday to Saturday I am based at the Sunderland office.

I hope to see you in the near future.

Yours sincerely

Susanne Beaumont

Enc

Copy: Adam Randall
        File

Student Name   Exercise 3B   Centre No

Exercise 3E

Student Name   Exercise 3E   Centre No

WORKING FROM HOME

The average worker spends 2 hours a day travelling to and from their employment - an additional 25% on top of working hours. In bad weather conditions, journeys can be long and very unpleasant and the dramatically rising levels of pollution have lead to an enormous increase in the incidence of asthma. The common cold, influenza and other virus infections spread rapidly in a stuffy working environment and poor ventilation can cause sinus troubles and headaches. The country currently loses over 400 million working days through sickness per year.

Research shows that going to work causes stress and even illness. A healthy business needs healthy staff but workers are actually being made ill by factors such as traffic chaos, accidents, transport strikes and delays.

A report by a management consultant for a group of employers suggests that the solution is to allow people to work from home - 'teleworking' is the term used to describe this. It has been shown that teleworkers take less time off sick and do an average of 45% more work.

It is estimated that almost 2 million people are now working from home in Britain and they spend more than 50% of their time in doing so. They can go into the office after the rush hour and at times to suit them.

Approximately 7 in 10 employers will try teleworking before the end of the century as developments in information technology make links between home and office more sophisticated.

TELEWORKING

Student Name   Exercise 3C   Centre No

Electronic mail (E-mail) is the key to teleworking. Documents can be written and transmitted without the use of paper. Messages can be sent at any time - locations and time zones do not need to be taken into consideration as the communication is stored on the computer until the 'mailbox' is opened by the individual concerned.

TELEWORKING

2

Exercise 3F

Student Name   Exercise 3F   Centre No

TELEWORKING

<u>WORKING FROM HOME</u>

The average worker spends 2 hours a day travelling to and from their employment - an additional 25% on top of working hours. In bad weather conditions, journeys can be long and very unpleasant and the dramatically rising levels of pollution have lead to an enormous increase in the incidence of asthma. The common cold, influenza and other virus infections spread rapidly in a stuffy working environment and poor ventilation can cause sinus troubles and headaches. The country currently loses over 400 million working days through sickness per year.

Research shows that going to work causes stress and even illness. A healthy business needs healthy staff but workers are actually being made ill by factors such as traffic chaos, accidents, transport strikes and delays.

A report by a management consultant for a group of employers suggests that the solution is to allow people to work from home - 'teleworking' is the term used to describe this. It has been shown that teleworkers take less time off sick and do an average of 45% more work.

It is estimated that almost 2 million people are now working from home in Britain and they spend more than 50% of their time in doing so. They can go into the office after the rush hour and at times to suit them.

Approximately 7 in 10 employers will try teleworking before the end of the century as developments in information technology make links between home and office more sophisticated.

01/01/95   10:30

Student Name   Exercise 3E   Centre No

Electronic mail (E-mail) is the key to teleworking. Documents can be written and transmitted without the use of paper. Messages can be sent at any time - locations and time zones do not need to be taken into consideration as the communication is stored on the computer until the 'mailbox' is opened by the individual concerned.

<u>WORKING FROM HOME</u>

There are advantages to both employers and employees.

<u>Advantages to the Employer</u>

Reduced office costs and overheads

Improved productivity

Retention of key staff

Less absence through sickness

<u>Advantages to the Employee</u>

Avoids travel stress

Arranges own working hours

Better for disabled workers

Childcare can be combined (to some extent)

Less contact with infectious diseases

As the needs of business and workers develop and technology becomes available, teleworking is a very realistic option. In the near future, many of us will not only be able to shop and be entertained from home, we will also be able to work from home.

TELEWORKING

2

Task 4A

❖❖❖❖❖❖❖❖❖❖   ❖❖❖❖❖❖❖❖❖❖

VINE TREE COLLEGE

GRAPE LANE
GLASSINGTON
YORK YO6 9RW

TEL: 0904-66542 FAX: 0904-34534

Our ref CBD/VF/accom2

date of typing

URGENT

Ms Helen Forsyth
3A Maple Avenue West
Chestnut Park
ROYAL LEAMINGTON SPA
Warwickshire
CV31 8PA

Dear Ms Forsyth

Thank you for your application for the Cordon Bleu Diploma course which will be duly processed by our Admissions Tutor.

I am writing in response to your letter in which you requested information about the type of accommodation available to full-time students. The College is situated just outside the old, walled City of York in an attractive, rural setting near to the River Ouse. Students are housed in 2-storey blocks surrounding a central courtyard. Ample car/bike parking is provided adjacent to the accommodation blocks.

Each room is centrally-heated, fully-furnished and has an en-suite bathroom. Self-catering kitchens are shared by approximately 6 students. An illustrated brochure is enclosed.

Accommodation can be booked by completing the enclosed form and returning it to me, preferably before the end of *(last day of next month)*. You should clearly state your preference for a smoking/non-smoking, single/mixed-sex block.

Yours sincerely

Veronique Flaubert
Accommodation Officer

Encs

Student Name   Exercise 3F   Centre No

TELEWORKING

Electronic mail (E-mail) is the key to teleworking. Documents can be written and transmitted without the use of paper. Messages can be sent at any time - locations and time zones do not need to be taken into consideration as the communication is stored on the computer until the 'mailbox' is opened by the individual concerned.

WORKING FROM HOME

There are advantages to both employers and employees.

Advantages to the Employer

Reduced office costs and overheads

Improved productivity

Retention of key staff

Less absence through sickness

Advantages to the Employee

Avoids travel stress

Arranges own working hours

Better for disabled workers

Childcare can be combined (to some extent)

Less contact with infectious diseases

As the needs of business and workers develop and technology becomes available, teleworking is a very realistic option. In the near future, many of us will not only be able to shop and be entertained from home, we will also be able to work from home.

2   01/01/95   10:30

The full time course is composed of six modules, each of which may be studied separately on a part time basis. Completion of all six modules leads to the award of the College's CERTIFICATE IN CORDON BLEU COOKERY, and some of the modules will be accredited by national assessment and examining boards.

Attendance on part time programmes is from 1.00 pm to 9.00 pm on one day per week for one term. Part time students will be expected to produce written assignments and evidence of practical work done outside College, and therefore should be already employed in the Catering/Hotel industry. Prospective students are invited to discuss this aspect with a tutor before enrolment.

Modular Programme

Wines and Spirits

Wine tasting, labelling, viniculture.

Floral Art

Selection and care of foliage, flowers and herbs. Colour, design, table and room settings.

Interior Decor

Selection and co-ordination of fabrics and accessories. The use of lighting and styles to achieve effects.

Business Skills

The setting-up and successful operation of food-based enterprises.

Food Hygiene

A programme leading to a nationally recognised qualification.

European Study Tour

An opportunity to compare skills and techniques - and to enjoy the culture, food and wines.

Prospects for Career Progression

2

Task 4B

VINE TREE COLLEGE
CULINARY ARTS COURSES

The College offers residential accommodation in an attractive, rural setting just outside York.

The workrooms and the Training Restaurant are fully-fitted with the latest up-to-date specialist equipment.

Because of the practical nature of the courses, and the need for personal tuition and creative development, we have set a maximum number of ten students on all programmes, including the full time Diploma.

Former students have been successful in obtaining employment in restaurants both in this country and abroad. Some students have continued into higher education.

CORDON BLEU DIPLOMA

A one-year full time programme leading to the College's Diploma in Cordon Bleu Cookery. The Diploma is a well-respected qualification throughout the country. Assessment is continuous throughout the year and consists of practical and written assignments. A final examination is taken in June. Successful students will be accredited with a nationally recognised qualification in Professional Cookery.

Students will acquire a thorough grounding in basic principles and skills and then progress to advanced culinary techniques.

In addition to the food preparation module, students will gain knowledge and skills in spirits and wines, interior decor, floral art, business skills and food hygiene. A study tour in a European country (normally Belgium, France or Italy) is an optional part of the programme, and one which students find both enjoyable and informative.

Task 4D

VINE TREE COLLEGE
CULINARY ARTS COURSES

The Vine Tree College offers residential accommodation in an attractive, rural setting just outside York. The workrooms and the Training Restaurant are fully-fitted with the latest up-to-date specialist equipment.

Because of the practical nature of the courses, and the need for personal tuition and creative development, we have set a maximum number of ten students on all programmes, including the full time Diploma.

Former students have been successful in obtaining employment in restaurants both in this country and abroad. Some students have continued into higher education.

CORDON BLEU DIPLOMA

A one-year full time programme leading to the Vine Tree College's Diploma in Cordon Bleu Cookery. The Diploma is a well-respected qualification throughout the country. Assessment is continuous throughout the year and consists of practical and written assignments. A final examination is taken in June. Successful students will be accredited with a nationally recognised qualification in Professional Cookery.

Students will acquire a thorough grounding in basic principles and skills and then progress to advanced culinary techniques.

In addition to the food preparation module, students will gain knowledge and skills in spirits and wines, interior decor, floral art, business skills and food hygiene. A study tour in a European country (normally Belgium, France or Italy) is an optional part of the programme, and one which students find both enjoyable and informative.

Task 4C

MEMORANDUM

TO: Dave Collingridge, Services Unit

FROM: Veronique Flaubert, Accommodation Officer

REF: VF/SU/9503

DATE: *Date of typing*

BY HAND

I understand that you have already been approached by several of our students with reference to the central heating in Ebor block.

It appears that there is a problem with the timing of the system in that the heating has been coming on between 10.00 am and 6.00 pm whilst students are attending courses. When the students return to their rooms between 5.00 pm and 5.30 pm, the temperature is unbearably hot - particularly in good weather. However, by 10.00 pm the rooms are beginning to cool down and, during the night, many students said they have found it too cold to sleep.

This inefficient operation and use of resources is to the general detriment of the College, and I would be obliged if you could make every effort to amend the situation. It seems that two issues need to be addressed - the timing and the thermostatic control of the system. Students have approached the Principal on this matter and so I have sent her a copy of this memo.

Please keep me informed of progress.

Copy: The Principal

Exercise 5B

M E M O R A N D U M

FROM: Jim Watson, Personnel

TO: Lesley Huntington, Reception

REF: JW/CC3/72R

DATE: today's

Staff extension numbers

As you are aware, there have been several changes in staffing recently and this has affected some staff telephone extension numbers.

The following staff are now available on telephone extension numbers:

Rothery, Mavis	2119
Bush, Martin	2124
Whitaker, David	2147
Allingham, Mark	2211
Wade, Christine	2347
Bell, Susan	2422
Watson, Mary	2665
Greenwood, Joyce	2831

The following are new staff to the company and are allocated temporary extension numbers:

Lighthowler, John	3001
Simpson, Dee	3002
Ali, Riaz	3003

Until the new telephone extension booklet is reproduced next month, can you please alert all Reception and Switchboard staff of the changes.

The full time course is composed of six modules, each of which may be studied separately on a part time basis. Completion of all six modules leads to the award of the Vine Tree College's CERTIFICATE IN CORDON BLEU COOKERY, and some of the modules will be accredited by national assessment and examining boards.

Attendance on part time programmes is from 1.00 pm to 9.00 pm on one day per week for one term. Part time students will be expected to produce written assignments and evidence of practical work done outside Vine Tree College, and therefore should be already employed in the Catering/Hotel industry. Prospective students are invited to discuss this aspect with a tutor before enrolment.

Modular Programme

Wines and Spirits

Wine tasting, labelling, viniculture.

Floral Art

Selection and care of foliage, flowers and herbs. Colour, design, table and room settings.

Interior Decor

Selection and co-ordination of fabrics and accessories. The use of lighting and styles to achieve effects.

Business Skills

The setting-up and successful operation of food-based enterprises.

Food Hygiene

A programme leading to a nationally recognised qualification.

European Study Tour

An opportunity to compare skills and techniques - and to enjoy the culture, food and wines.

Prospects for Career Progression

Former students of the Vine Tree College have obtained varied and interesting employment in the running of restaurants, teaching adult classes, private catering and freelance chalet/yachting services.

Students wishing to enter higher education in the field of food technology have combined their studies with 'A' levels.

'Old' students regularly return to Vine Tree College classrooms to pass on their experiences (usually informative, often hilarious) to our current Diploma and Certificate students.

For further information, please ring the Vine Tree College Information Centre on 0904-661942.

Exercise 5C

M E M O R A N D U M

FROM: Jim Watson, Personnel

TO: Lesley Huntington, Reception

REF: JW/CC3/72R

DATE: today's

Staff extension numbers

As you are aware, there have been several changes in staffing recently and this has affected some staff telephone extension numbers.

The following staff are now available on telephone extension numbers:

Allingham, Mark	2211
Bell, Susan	2422
Bush, Martin	2124
Greenwood, Joyce	2831
Rothery, Mavis	2119
Wade, Christine	2347
Watson, Mary	2665
Whitaker, David	2147

The following are new staff to the company and are allocated temporary extension numbers:

Ali, Riaz	3003
Lighthowler, John	3001
Simpson, Dee	3002

Until the new telephone extension booklet is reproduced next month, can you please alert all Reception and Switchboard staff of the changes.

Exercise 5D

M E M O R A N D U M

FROM: Jim Watson, Personnel

TO: Lesley Huntington, Reception

REF: JW/CC3/72R

DATE: today's

STAFF EXTENSION NUMBERS

As you are aware, there have been several changes in staffing recently and this has affected some staff telephone extension numbers. The following staff are now available on telephone extension numbers:

DEPARTMENT	NAME	EXT NO
Administration	Whitaker, David	2147
Catering	Wade, Christine	2347
Computing	Lighthowler, John	3001
Marketing	Ali, Riaz	3003
Personnel	Rothery, Mavis	2119
Purchasing	Simpson, Dee	3002
Reception	Bush, Martin	2124
Sales	Bell, Susan	2422
Sales	Watson, Mary	2665
Stores	Allingham, Mark	2211
Text Production	Greenwood, Joyce	2831

UNTIL THE NEW TELEPHONE EXTENSION BOOKLET IS REPRODUCED NEXT MONTH, CAN YOU PLEASE ALERT ALL RECEPTION AND SWITCHBOARD STAFF OF THE CHANGES.

Exercise 6B

FIRTH'S FANCY GOODS

ADDITIONAL STOCK COMMODITIES

ITEM	CAT NO	PRICE £	UNIT
Cruet Sets			
Cut-glass cruet	CRCG445	12.99	set
Pine cruet	CRPI444	3.99	set
Pottery cruet	CRPO443	5.99	set
Silver cruet	CRSI442	14.99	set
Cutlery			
Onyx-handled steak knives	SKOH723	25.99	set of 8
Silver cake slicer	CSSI721	14.99	each
Silver salad servers	SSSI722	21.99	pair
Silver steak knives	SKSI724	49.99	set of 8

Exercise 6C

NEW BEDLINEN ITEMS

We have recently introduced a new selection of bedlinens into our range. In order to promote sales, they will be offered at the special discount prices shown in the table below:

BEDLINEN ITEM	SIZE	ITEM CODE	COLOUR(S) AVAILABLE	PRICE OF ITEM USUAL £	SPECIAL £
Quilt Covers					
Zenith	SINGLE	QS241	red/white	18.99	16.99
Harlequin Court	DOUBLE	QD174	multi	29.99	24.99
Country Blossom	DOUBLE	QD183	rose	34.99	29.99
Pillowcases					
Zenith	N/A	P243	red/white	5.99	5.50
Harlequin Court	N/A	P176	multi	6.99	5.99
Country Blossom	N/A	P185	rose	7.99	6.99
Valances					
Zenith	SINGLE	VS242	red/white	16.99	14.99
Harlequin Court	DOUBLE	CD175	multi	26.99	21.99
Country Blossom	DOUBLE	VD184	rose	29.99	26.99

The "special" prices will be offered until the end of next month and then the usual price will apply.

Exercise 7B

Firths Fancy Goods
147 Stanningley Road
LEEDS
LO3 4TR

Tel No: 0532 672471

today's date

Mr B Waverley
Glen Cottage
Glen Crescent
BURNLEY
BR5 2LN

Dear Mr Waverley

Re: your order of 22 November 1994

We were pleased to receive your recent order for a selection of our fancy goods.

The goods you have requested are:

a)   l earthenware breadcrock @ £7.99 each.

b)   2 silver cruet sets @ £14.99 set.

The goods you have requested are in stock and will be despatched within the next fourteen days.

Thank you for your payment by cheque a receipt for which is enclosed with this letter.

Please find enclosed our new price list and latest catalogue. We look forward to offering our services to you again in the near future.

Yours sincerely
FIRTHS FANCY GOODS

Sales Department

Encs

Exercise 6D

WORK EXPERIENCE

TRAINEE DETAILS

If any trainees are unable to complete their work experience on the dates shown they should notify their Course Tutor immediately

NAME OF TRAINEE	ENROLMENT CODE	NAME OF ORGANISATION	WORK EXPERIENCE DATES START	FINISH
Art and Design				
DENT, Sally	34117	Century Graphics	7 Oct	18 Oct
HUGHES, Amy	36299	V J Designs Ltd	14 Oct	18 Oct
IQBAL, Abdul	36221	Jay's Art Decor	31 Oct	4 Nov
Business Studies				
ASHTON, Joe	37229	Haye & Lund Ltd	7 Oct	18 Oct
BRAY, Anthony	36121	Haye & Lund Ltd	14 oct	18 Oct
DAWLEY, Lisa	36145	William Dykes	21 Oct	28 Oct
JARVIS, Rita	33345	B Simms	7 Oct	18 Oct
MILNES, Mary	34276	B R Stubbs Ltd	14 Oct	18 Oct
SINGH, Jared	35127	J Spencer & Son	14 Oct	18 Oct
Catering				
BROWN, Sheila	35227	Verdi's Restaurant	7 Nov	18 Nov
HAIGH, Paula	36672	Astoria Hotel	31 Oct	4 Nov
TOWNSEND, Paul	35219	Susi's Bistro	31 Nov	4 Nov
WATTS, Evie	36761	Richmond Hotel	7 Nov	11 Nov

Exercise 7C

Firths Fancy Goods
147 Stanningley Road
LEEDS
LO3 4TR

Tel No: 0532 672471

today's date

Mrs L Anwar
37 Burberry Place
BURBERRY
BB5 4TL

Dear Mrs Anwar

We were pleased to receive your recent order for a selection of our fancy goods.

Your order included:

a)   1 set of onyx-handled steak knives @ £25.99 per set of 8.

b)   3 satin-edged hand towels in blue @ £4.99 each.

We regret to advise you that the goods are currently out of stock.

It seems that your order was taken from an out of date catalogue. Please find enclosed our new price list and latest catalogue.

We will be pleased to supply you with alternative items from the new catalogue or offer you a full refund.

Please accept our apologies for any inconvenience caused, along with the **attached £2 voucher** which you may use towards the cost of your replacement goods.

Yours sincerely
FIRTHS FANCY GOODS

Sales Department

Encs

Exercise 7D

Firths Fancy Goods
147 Stanningley Road
LEEDS
LO3 TR4

Tel No: 0532 672471

today's date

David Webb & Sons
Merdale Road
SKIPTON
SK9 4PT

Dear Sirs

Thank you for your recent enquiry regarding our range of fancy goods.

We are pleased to hear of your plans to refurbish your offices and to equip these with co-ordinating desk furniture.

Please find enclosed our new price list and latest catalogue. These give full details of the different ranges we can supply.

We would be able to offer you a **discount of 10%** on any order totalling more than £250. For orders over £500 a special discount can be negotiated - please contact Susan Bell on Extension 2422 for more details.

Yours faithfully
FIRTHS FANCY GOODS

Sales Department

Encs

Copy to: Susan Bell
         File

> Your copies of the letter should indicate the routeing:
>
> *(1st copy)*
> Copy to: Susan Bell✓
>   File
> *(2nd copy)*
> Copy to: Susan Bell
>   File✓

Task 8C

STAFF TRAINING

MEMORANDUM

FROM: Tony McFarlane, Personnel Manager

TO: Mariah Helliwell

REF: tm/sd/7342

DATE: today's

STAFF TRAINING APPLICATION

Thank you for your recent application for staff training.

I acknowledge that you are particularly interested in work-shadowing opportunities and am pleased to inform you that I have held discussions with Harry Browne, Senior Marketing Manager, and he has agreed to allow you to spend one day a week with him next month to gain some experience in marketing techniques.

I will recommend to Harry Browne that he should arrange for a meeting with yourself and your line manager in order to negotiate a mutually suitable day each week for the training to take place

In order to process your application, could you please complete the green Form STA/4, for which you will also need the signature of your line manager. Please let me have sight of the completed form as soon as possible.

We have a number of open learning packages which you can work through at your own pace using a PC.

Topics which I believe may be of particular interest to you include:

         Assertiveness training

         Computer applications

         Decision making

         Effective time management

         Financial planning techniques

         Industrial relations

         Managing human resources

         Operations management

         Organisation analysis

Task 8B

MEMORANDUM

FROM: Tony McFarlane, Personnel Manager

TO: Mariah Helliwell

REF: tm/sd/7342

DATE: today's

STAFF TRAINING APPLICATION

Thank you for your recent application for staff training.

I acknowledge that you are particularly interested in work-shadowing opportunities and am pleased to inform you that I have held discussions with Harold Brown, Senior Marketing Manager, and he has agreed to allow you to spend one day a week with him next month to gain some experience in marketing techniques.

In order to process your application, could you please complete the green Form STA/4, for which you will also need the signature of your line manager. Please let me have sight of the completed form as soon as possible.

We have a number of open learning packages which you can work through at your own pace using a PC.

Topics which I believe may be of particular interest to you include:

         Managing human resources
         Assertiveness training
         Financial planning techniques
         Effective time management
         Organisation analysis
         Computer applications
         Decision making
         Operations management
         Industrial relations

I will recommend to Harold Brown that he should arrange for a meeting with yourself and your line manager in order to negotiate a mutually suitable day each week for the training to take place.

Your copies of the memo should indicate the routeing:

(1st copy)   *(2nd copy)*
Copy to: Harold Brown ✔   Copy to: Harold Brown
          File   File ✔

Task 8D

STAFF TRAINING SESSIONS

DRAFT FOR MARCH

TRAINING SESSION	CODE	VENUE/ROOM	DATE	TRAINING SESSION TIMES START	FINISH
I.T. APPLICATIONS					
Introduction to CD-Rom	IT50	A42	8 March	1.30 pm	5.00 pm
Networking	IT47	A29	15 March	9.00 am	5.00 pm
Database	IT49	A29	22 March	9.00 am	12.30 pm
Advanced DTP	IT48	A29	29 March	9.00 am	5.00 pm
ADMINISTRATIVE					
Switchboard Training	A34	Reception	9 March	9.00 am	12.30 pm
Management Up-date	A33	Conference	21 March	1.30 pm	5.00 pm
Audio Training Day	A32	Main Office	28 March	9.00 am	5.00 pm
MISCELLANEOUS					
Assertiveness Training	M63	Boardroom	3 March	9.00 am	12.30 pm
Health and Safety	M62	Boardroom	10 March	9.00 am	12.30 pm
Public Speaking	M64	Conference	17 March	1.30 pm	5.00 pm
Time Organisation	M65	Conference	30 March	1.30 pm	5.00 pm

NB: Please note that Training Session A34, Switchboard Training, is for the switchboard system to be installed in April - training is, therefore, restricted to the Reception Team only.

STAFF TRAINING

If next month is inconvenient for your training to take place, I would suggest that you take the following action:

a) notify your line manager immediately

b) indicate on Form STA/4 an alternative date, or

c) call to see me personally to discuss your requirements

tm/sd/7342

2

Task 9C

Tower Computers

19 Greendale Road
HALIFAX
Tel No: 0422 378541

Our ref GJ/72f

today's date

URGENT

Miss Jane Hunter
42 Appleby Road
BATH
BA8 4GT

Dear Miss Hunter

I have received your recent enquiry about purchasing a computer from our company.

Our basic philosophy is to take every possible step to match all aspects of our business with customer satisfaction.

I am delighted to hear that you consider us to be a leading manufacturer in the computing field. I will try to let you have as much information as possible. We like to give our clients every opportunity to select the most appropriate equipment for their needs and at the expense they can best afford. Our entire range of products provides the best value for money and performance available.

All our systems carry a 12-month warranty for parts and labour including collection from, and return to, your own home.

One of our Sales Representatives, Simon De Vere, will be in your area soon and would be able to make an appointment to see you on *(date for first Monday of next month)*. Simon would be able to demonstrate several models in your own home.

As we are a British company with over 20 years' experience in the computing industry, you can trust in our proven record of providing reliable and quality services.

In the meantime, please find enclosed this year's new catalogue with details of our full range of systems along with a number of miscellaneous products.

Yours sincerely

Gareth Jones
Sales Administrator

Enc

Task 9B

Tower Computers

19 Greendale Road
HALIFAX
Tel No: 0422 378541

Our ref GJ/72f

today's date

URGENT

Miss Jane Hunter
42 Appleby Road
BATH
BA8 4GT

Dear Miss Hunter

I have received your recent enquiry about purchasing a computer from our company.

I am delighted to hear that you consider us to be a leading manufacturer in the computing field. I will try to let you have as much information as possible. We like to give our clients every opportunity to select the most appropriate equipment for their needs and at the expense they can best afford.

One of our Sales Representatives, Simon De Vere, will be in your area soon and would be able to make an appointment to see you on *(date for first Monday of next month)*. Simon would be able to demonstrate several models in your own home.

In the meantime, please find enclosed this year's new catalogue with details of our full range of systems along with a number of miscellaneous products.

Yours sincerely

Gareth Jones
Sales Administrator

Enc

Task 9E

COMPUTER HARDWARE

SOME 'INSIDE' INFORMATION

There are now numerous clones of the IBM PC on the market and faced with such a wide choice, it's often difficult for the average consumer to know what specifications to look for.

Purchasing the wrong hardware and software could be a costly business so it's worth spending some time checking out the basic details.

PROCESSOR

The processor is important because it determines the speed at which your system will operate. For modern software you will need at least a 386 processor, although a 486 or better would be preferable. Remember also that a DX machine is faster than an SX.

Another factor affecting speed is the 'clock speed' usually quoted in megahertz (MHz). This indicates the number of software instructions that the processor can handle per second. The more the MHz the faster the processor will run.

PROCESSOR UPGRADEABLE

With technology moving so rapidly, it can be worth considering a 'processor-upgradeable' PC - the processor is mounted in a removable card which can be traded in later for something more powerful. A disadvantage is that they can be very expensive.

Task 9D

MEMORANDUM

From: Gareth Jones, Sales Administrator

To: Zandra Holstedt, Rep Supervisor

Ref: GJ/SR/47

Date: today's

SALES REP VISITS

Following a number of customer enquiries received recently, I have arranged for sales rep appointments to take place on the dates shown in the table below. If any dates are inconvenient please let me know as soon as possible through normal channels so that I may have sufficient time to arrange an alternative date with the customer.

CUSTOMER NAME	CUSTOMER ADDRESS DETAILS STREET/ROAD etc	TOWN	TELEPHONE NO	DATE
Rep: Lydia Austin				
Dobson, Marie	2 Kirkdale Road	MIRFIELD	0924 347718	22/*/**
Fenney, Ian	58 Astral Avenue	MIRFIELD	0924 677541	12/*/**
James, William	20 Bethel Street	GRIMSBY	0472 358211	19/*/**
Shafiq, Mohammed	62 Turner View	GRIMSBY	0472 566222	13/*/**
Rep: Simon De Vere				
Hunter, Jane	42 Appleby Road	BATH	0225 577711	(as Task 9B)
Leigh, Vera	26 Scarbottom Road	BURY	0798 364792	26/*/**
Middleton, Sam	49 Highway Crescent	LEEDS	0532 579241	7/*/**
Nazir, Ashraf	14 Regents Close	BURY	0798 465232	9/*/**
Rep: Mila Yokovic				
Grimes, Henry	77 Lister Road	YORK	0904 621721	17/*/**
Roberts, Jan	17 Exmoor Street	YORK	0904 497733	8/*/**
Wood, Jordan	9 Waverley Place	YORK	0904 562214	27/*/**

NB: the dates in this column should be displayed with name of next month and this year in the format of dd/mm/yy, e.g. 25/10/95

Task 9F

BASIC SYSTEM INFORMATION

COMPUTER HARDWARE

SOME 'INSIDE' INFORMATION

Purchasing the wrong hardware and software could be a costly business so it's worth spending some time checking out the basic details.

There are now numerous clones of the IBM Personal Computer on the market and faced with such a wide choice, it's often difficult for the average consumer to know what specifications to look for.

HARD DISK

A hard disk is usually 'fixed' inside the Personal Computer and provides permanent storage for programs and data. The storage capacity of a hard disk is measured in megabytes (Mb). One megabyte can store approximately a million characters of text, numbers or program code etc.

That may seem excessive, but when you realise that a single advanced software program can easily eat up 5Mb-10Mb before you even begin to work on it, it's easy to see how you could soon fill a 40Mb hard disk. In the long run it makes good sense to buy the best hard disk you can afford.

HARD DISK

A hard disk is usually 'fixed' inside the PC and provides permanent storage for programs and data. The storage capacity of a hard disk is measured in megabytes (Mb).

One megabyte can store approximately a million characters of text, numbers or program code etc.

That may seem a lot, but when you realise that a single advanced application can easily eat up 5Mb-10Mb before you even begin to work on it, it's easy to see how you could soon fill a 40Mb hard disk. Although it's possible to upgrade, it's both costly and disruptive.

2

BASIC SYSTEM INFORMATION

SCREENS

Nowadays, VGA (video graphics adapter) is the minimum screen display to select with its image of 640 by 48 points (pixels) in 16 colours or 320 by 200 points in 256 colours. Although VGA is good enough for most users, you can get SVGA (SuperVGA) with even higher resolutions of around 1024 by 768 and more colours.

If you are buying on a shoestring, you can save money with a monochrome screen - most applications don't need to be run in colour.

Purchasing the wrong software and hardware could be a costly business so it's worth spending some time checking out the basic details.

3

BASIC SYSTEM INFORMATION

PROCESSOR

The processor should be a prime factor because it determines the speed at which your system will operate. For modern software you will need at least a 386 processor, although a 486 or better would be preferable. Remember also that a DX machine is faster than an SX.

Another factor affecting speed is the 'clock speed' usually quoted in megahertz (MHz). This indicates the number of software instructions that the processor can handle per second. The more the MHz the faster the processor will run.

PROCESSOR UPGRADEABLE

With technology moving so rapidly, it may be worth considering a 'processor-upgradeable' Personal Computer. A disadvantage is that they can be very expensive.

MEMORY

Random access memory (RAM) is necessary to store programs and data whilst they are in use. Memory is also measured in Mb and if you are using Microsoft Windows you need a lot of it! Ideally a well-designed Personal Computer should have room to expand to 32 Mb or even 64 Mb, with at least 8 Mb on the main board.

2

Progress review checklist

Unit	Topic	Date completed	Comments
1	Typescript containing typographical and spelling errors		
	Typescript containing correction signs		
	Typescript containing abbreviations		
	Changing the line length		
	Proof-reading		
2	Business letter layout		
	Consistency of presentation		
	Locating information in another document		
	Memorandum layout		
	Documents with continuation sheet		
	Page numbering (insert method)		
	Printing on letterhead		
	Routeing of copies		
3	Headers and footers		
	Page numbering (header and footer method)		
	Formatting requirements		
	Organizing text editing		
	Moving around the document – quick methods		
	Deleting text – quick method		
4	Consolidation 1		
5	Sorting (rearranging) items		
	Changing case		
6	Normal tabulation procedures – general information		
	Creating tables – using normal tabulation facilities		
	Creating tables – using Word's table facilities and Table Wizard:: • setting tabs • moving around in a table • changing column width • changing row height • inserting/deleting columns • inserting/deleting rows • merging/splitting cells		
	Subdivided and multi-line column headings		
7	Boilerplating using standard files		
	Boilerplating using AutoText		
8	Consolidation 2		
9	Examination practice		

Glossary

Action ☞	Keyboard ⌨	Mouse 🖱	Menu 📄
Allocate clear lines	Press: ↵ once for each line required, plus one		
Allocate vertical space			Format, Paragraphs Key in measurement
AutoText			
Create an AutoText entry	n/a	Key in and select text to be stored Click: 🖼 on Standard Tool Bar Name the entry. Click: **Add**	Key in and select text to be stored Select: **Edit**, **AutoText** Name the entry. Click: **Add**
Insert an AutoText entry	Position insertion point Type: **Name** of AutoText entry Press: **F3**	Position insertion point Type: **Name** of AutoText entry Click: 🖼 on Standard Tool Bar	Position insertion point Select: **Edit**, **AutoText** Click: Insert button
Blocked capitals	Press: **Caps lock** key		
Boilerplating	*See* AutoText *or* Standard paragraph files		
Bold text	Press: **Ctrl + B**	Click: **B** on Formatting Tool Bar	Format, Font
Bulleted lists		Click: 📋 on Formatting Tool Bar	Format, Bullets and Numbering
Case of letters	Press: **Shift + F3** To capitalize letters: Press: **Ctrl + Shift + A**		Format, Change case
Centre text	Press: **Ctrl + E**	Click: ▦ on Formatting Tool Bar	Format, Paragraphs, Indents and Spacing, Alignment
Close a file (clear screen)	Press: **Ctrl + C**		File, Close
Copy a block of text			
Select text to be copied	Press: **Ctrl + C**	Click: 📋 on Standard Tool Bar *or* Press: Right mouse button and Select: **Copy**	Edit, Copy
Position cursor where text is to be copied to	Press: **Ctrl + V**	Click: 📋 on Standard Tool Bar *or* Press: Right mouse button and select: **Paste**	Edit, Paste
Cursor movement			
Move cursor to required position	Use arrow keys ↑ ↓ ← →	Click: Left mouse button in required position	
Move to top of document	**Ctrl + Home**		
Move to end of document	**Ctrl + End**		
Move left word by word	**Ctrl + ←**		
Move right word by word	**Ctrl + →**		
Move to end of line	**End**		
Move to start of line	**Home**		
Cut text	*See* Delete/cut a block of text		
Date insertion	Press: **Alt + Shift + D**		Insert, Date and Time
Delete a character	Move cursor to incorrect character: Press: **Del** *or* Move cursor to right of incorrect character: Press ← (Del)		
Delete a word	Move cursor to end of word: Press: **Ctrl + ← (Del)** *or* **Ctrl + X**	Double-click on word to select: Press: Right mouse button Select: **Cut**	Select: **Edit**, **Cut**
Delete/cut a block of text	Select incorrect text: Press: ← (Del) *or* select word: Press: **Ctrl + X**	Select incorrect text: Press: Right mouse button Select: **Cut**	Select incorrect text: Select: **Edit**, **Cut**
Exit the program	Press: **Alt + F4**	Double-click control button at left of title bar	File, Exit
Find text	Press: **Ctrl + F**		Edit, Find
Font size	Press: **Ctrl + Shift + P** Choose desired size	Click: 10 ▾ on Formatting Tool Bar Choose desired size	Format, Font Choose desired size
Next larger point size	Press: **Ctrl +]**		
Next smaller point size	Press: **Ctrl + [**		
Font typeface style	Press: **Ctrl + Shift + F** Choose desired font	Click: Times New Roman ▾ on Formatting Tool Bar Choose desired font	Format, Font Choose desired font

Action ☞	Keyboard ⌨	Mouse ⌐	Menu ▤
Footers			<u>V</u>iew, <u>H</u>eader and Footer
			Click: Switch between header and footer button. Key in footer text
			Click on **OK**
To delete a footer			<u>V</u>iew, <u>H</u>eader and Footer
			Select: Text in footer box and delete
Go to (a specified page)	Press: **Ctrl + G**		<u>E</u>dit, <u>G</u>o To ...
	or **F5**		
Grammar tool			<u>T</u>ools, <u>G</u>rammar
Headers			<u>V</u>iew, <u>H</u>eader and Footer
			Key in header text. Click on OK
To delete a header			<u>V</u>iew, <u>H</u>eader and Footer
			Select: Text in header box and delete
Help function	Press: **F1** (for contents)	Click: 🔽 on Formatting Tool Bar	<u>H</u>elp
	Press: **Shift + F1**		
	(for context sensitive help)		
Indent function			
Indent at left to next tab stop	Press: **Ctrl + M**	Click: ▦ on Formatting Tool Bar	<u>F</u>ormat, <u>P</u>aragraphs, <u>I</u>ndents and Spacing
Indent at left to previous tab stop	Press: **Ctrl + Shift + M**		
Indent as a hanging paragraph	Press: **Ctrl + T**		
Unindent and return to standard margins	Press: **Ctrl + Q**	Click: ▦ on Formatting Tool Bar	
		using ruler:	
		First-line indent	
		Left indent	
		First-line and left indents	
		Right indent	
Insert a line break	Press: **Shift + ↵**		
Insert a page break	Press: **Ctrl + ↵**		<u>I</u>nsert, <u>B</u>reak, Page break
Insert special characters/symbols	Press: **Ctrl + Shift + Q**		Position cursor where you want the character/symbol to appear:
			Select: <u>I</u>nsert, <u>S</u>ymbol
Insert text	Simply key in the missing character(s) at the appropriate place – the existing text will 'move over' to make room for the new text.		
Italics	Press: **Ctrl + I**	Click: *I* on Formatting Tool Bar	<u>F</u>ormat, <u>F</u>ont
Justified right margin	Press: **Ctrl + J**	Click: ▤ on Formatting Tool Bar	<u>F</u>ormat, <u>P</u>aragraphs, <u>I</u>ndents and Spacing, Alignment
Line length – to change	Select text. Display horizontal ruler. Move margin markers to required position on ruler.		
Line spacing – to set	Press: **Ctrl + 1** (single)		<u>F</u>ormat, <u>P</u>aragraphs, <u>I</u>ndents and Spacing
	Press: **Ctrl + 2** (double)		
	Press: **Ctrl + 0** (to add or delete a line space)		
Margins (to change)			<u>F</u>ile, Page Setup, <u>M</u>argins
Move a block of text			
Select text to be moved	Press: **Ctrl + X** *or* **F2**	Click: ✂ on Standard Tool Bar	<u>E</u>dit, Cu<u>t</u>
Position cursor where text is to be moved to	Press: **Ctrl + V** *or* **↵**	Click: 📋 on Standard Tool Bar	<u>E</u>dit, <u>P</u>aste
	or Hold down **Ctrl** and	*Drag and drop moving:*	
	Click: Right mouse button	Select text to be moved	
		Click left mouse button in middle of text and keep held down	
		Drag selection to required location	
		Release mouse button	
Move around text quickly			
Left/right word by word	Press: **Ctrl + ←** *or* **Ctrl + →**		
End/start of line	Press: **End** *or* **Home**		
Top/bottom of paragraph	Press: **Ctrl + ↑** *or* **Ctrl + ↓**		
Up/down one screen	Press: **PgUp** *or* **PgDn**		
Top/bottom of document	Press: **Ctrl + Home**		
	or **Ctrl + End**		
Open an existing file	Press: **Ctrl + O**	Click: 📂 on Standard Tool Bar	<u>F</u>ile, <u>O</u>pen
Open a new file	Press: **Ctrl + N**	Click: ▢ on Standard Tool Bar	<u>F</u>ile, <u>N</u>ew
Page numbering	Press: **Alt + Shift + P**		<u>I</u>nsert, Page N<u>u</u>mbers
to delete page numbering			<u>V</u>iew, <u>H</u>eader and Footer
			Select the page numbers and delete

Action ☞	Keyboard	Mouse	Menu
Page Setup			**F**ile, **P**age Set**u**p (Choose from **Margins**, **Paper Size**, **Paper Source** and **Layout**)
Paragraphs – splitting/joining	Make a new paragraph (i.e. split a paragraph into two)	Move cursor to first letter of new paragraph Press: ↵ twice	
	Join two consecutive paragraphs into one	Move cursor to first character of second paragraph Press: ← (**Del**) twice (backspace delete key) Press: **Spacebar** (to insert a space after full stop)	
Print out hard copy	Press: **Ctrl + P**	Click: 🖨 on Standard Tool Bar	**F**ile, **Print**
Ragged right margin	Press: **Ctrl + L**	Click: 📄 on Formatting Tool Bar	**F**ormat, **P**aragraphs, **I**ndents and Spacing, Alignment
Remove text emphasis	Press: **Ctrl + Spacebar** *or* Press: **Ctrl + Shift + Z**	Select text to be changed back to normal text: Click: Appropriate button on Formatting Tool Bar	**F**ormat, **P**aragraphs, **I**ndents and Spacing
Repeating actions	Press: **F4** to repeat previous action *or* Press: **Ctrl + Y**	Click: 🔽 on Formatting Tool Bar	To repeat sets of actions, drag down the **Redo** drop-down list and select the group of actions you wish to repeat
Replace text – typeover	1 Select the incorrect text and then type in the correct entry – Word will fit the replacement text exactly into the original space 2 Move cursor to incorrect entry: Press: The **Ins** key (typeover on) and overtype with correct entry Press: The **Ins** key again (typeover off) to stop overtyping text		
Restore deleted text	Press: **Ctrl + Z**	Click: ↺ on Formatting Tool Bar	**E**dit, **U**ndo
Ruler – to display			**V**iew, **R**uler
Save work to disk Save a file for the first time	Press: **F12**		**F**ile, Save **A**s Enter **F**ilename Select correct **Directory** and **Drive** Click on **OK**
Save an active file which has been saved previously	Press: **Ctrl + S** *or* Press: **Shift + F12**	Click: 💾 on Standard Tool Bar	**F**ile, **S**ave
Save *all* open files			**F**ile, Save **All**
Scroll bars (to view)			**T**ools, **O**ptions, View Select: **Horizontal** scroll bar and **Vertical** scroll bar options
Search for text	*See* Find text.		
Select text One character (or more)	Press: **Shift + ←** *or* →	Click and drag pointer across text	
One word	Press: **Shift + Ctrl + ←** *or* →	Double-click on word	
To end of line	Press: **Shift + End**	Click and drag pointer right or down	
Start of line	Press: **Shift + Home**	Click and drag pointer left or up	
A full line	Press: **Shift + End** *or* **Home**	Click in selection border	
A paragraph	—	Double-click in selection border	
Whole document	Press: **Ctrl + A**	Triple-click in selection border	
Any block of text	—	Position pointer at start of text and Press: **Shift**. Then, position pointer at end of text and click	
Remove selection		Click in any white space	
Sort (rearrange items)			Select the items or text to be sorted Select: **T**able, **Sort**...
Spaced capitals	Press: **Caps lock** key. Leave one space after each letter. Leave three spaces after each word.		
Spellcheck	Press: **F7**	Click: 📝 on Standard Tool Bar	**T**ools, **S**pelling
Standard paragraph files	*To store standard paragraphs:* Key in the portion of text to be saved as a standard paragraph file – save it in a separate file using normal *save* procedures *To insert standard paragraphs into your document:* Position insertion point where you want the standard paragraph to be inserted. Select: **F**ile from the **I**nsert menu and select or key in the appropriate filename		
Status bar			**T**ools, Options, View Select: **Status B**ar option
Switch on and load Word		Double-click **Microsoft Word** icon	
Symbols	*See* Insert special characters/symbols.		

Action ☞	*Keyboard* ⌨	*Mouse* 🖰	*Menu* 📄
Tabulation	Select the paragraph(s) in which you wish to make changes to the tab settings, then either:		
	1 Select **T**abs from the **F**ormat menu		
	2 Click the tab marker on the horizontal ruler line to select the type of tab you want,		
	then drag the tab to the required position on the horizontal ruler line		
Remove tabs	(*note:* Drag a tab marker *off* the horizontal ruler line to remove it)		
Tables (*see also* Unit 6)		Click: 🔲 on Standard Tool Bar	**T**able, **I**nsert Table
Text, replace	Press: **Ctrl + H**		**E**dit, **R**eplace
Underline text	Press: **Ctrl + U**	Click: **U** on Formatting Tool Bar	F**o**rmat, **F**ont
Single word	Press: **Ctrl + Shift + W**		
Double word	Press: **Ctrl + Shift + H**		
Undoing actions	Press: **Ctrl + Z**	Click: ↺⏷ on Standard Tool Bar	To undo sets of actions, drag down the **Undo** drop-down list and select the group of actions you wish to undo
Units of measurement			**T**ools, **O**ptions, General **M**easurement Units Select desired units
View magnified pages		Click: 100% ⏷ on Standard Tool Bar Click: **Magnifies** on print preview	**V**iew, **Z**oom
View – normal view	Press: **Ctrl + F2**	Click: 🔳 **Normal** button at bottom left of document window	**V**iew, **N**ormal
View – outline view		Click: 📑 **Outline** button at bottom left of document window	**V**iew, **O**utline
View – page layout view		Click: 🔳 **Page Layout** button at bottom left of document window	**V**iew, **P**age Layout
View – print preview	Press: **Ctrl + F2**	Click: 🔍 on Standard Tool Bar	**F**ile, **P**rint Pre**v**iew
Widow/orphan protection			F**o**rmat, **P**aragraph, Text **F**low Check that the X is showing on the widow/orphan control box